Imprint Your Detection Dog in 15 Days

CW01084282

Cover photo: © Paul Bunker

Dedication

Over the years, I have trained or been involved with the training of hundreds and into the thousands of dogs. I have also had several dogs of my own that I actively work with. But of all the dogs, one has stood out as special. Ssaber was a "failed" military detection dog that just bonded with me from the first time I met him. When he came up for adoption at about 18 months old, I ended up buying a house, so I was allowed to take him home. For over ten years he was the best dog ever, and I miss him greatly. So, my first book I want to dedicate to the reason I share my life with dogs, which is that all the Ssaber's of this world make our lives feel special.

Ssaber
February 2008 – November 2020

"Everyone thinks they have the best dog...and none of them are wrong."
- W.R.Purche

Table of Contents

FOREWORD...**4**

BACKGROUND...**6**

INTRODUCTION..**7**

   WELFARE 8

TERMINOLOGY...**10**

CHAPTER 1 – HOW TO USE THIS BOOK **12**

   ROADMAP 15

   TRAINING PLAN, EXAMPLE LESSON 16

   TRAINING PLAN, EXAMPLE LESSON PG. 2 17

CHAPTER 2 – REWARD SELECTION..**19**

   TOY REWARD ASSESSMENT 28

CHAPTER 3 – CLICKER TRAINING..**35**

CHAPTER 4 – ODOR SELECTION **46**

CHAPTER 5 – ODOR STORAGE AND HANDLING..**53**

CHAPTER 6 – TEACHING THE RESPONSE **62**

CHAPTER 7 – METHOD OF IMPRINTING **81**

CHAPTER 8 – RECORD KEEPING **101**

CONCLUSION..**103**

REFERENCES **105**

ABOUT THE AUTHOR...**106**

CONNECT WITH THE AUTHOR **108**

FOREWORD

During my 20 years in the Marine Corps, I was fortunate to dedicate a majority of my career to the Military Working Dog (MWD) Program. Over the years, I served with some of the best handlers and trainers in the community and was humbled to be a part of an incredible generation of Marines who helped develop the MWD Program to counter the threats in Iraq and Afghanistan. My MWD career started in 1999 when our primary mission was law enforcement and force protection. After 9/11, we developed new MWD capabilities, implemented new training courses, and enhanced our overall mission readiness to ultimately save lives in combat. Improvised Explosive Devices (IED) were the number one threat to Coalition Forces and a well-trained dog team became one of most effective countermeasures.

Chris and SSD Lucca
© Chris Willingham

During one particular clearing operation in Iraq, my responsibility was to search a route just south of Baghdad. There had not been any sustained Coalition presence in the area in over nine months. It was an insurgent stronghold, and they were constantly attacking Baghdad with mortars and vehicle-borne IEDs. Our mission was to systematically search and clear the area and establish a presence to restrict insurgent freedom of movement. For this specific mission, we were tasked with clearing Route Gnat which ran north to south adjacent to the Tigris River. My assigned K-9 partner was a Specialized Search Dog (SSD) who was trained to search off-leash and locate explosive odor. We treated each choke point as a high-risk search and I would check the wind, which determined the side of the road I started on, and I would send my dog searching up the road to and through the choke point, then I would recall her on the same side of the route. Then, I would move to the opposite side of the route and search it in a similar fashion. While searching our third choke point, my SSD started displaying the undeniable change of behavior she had when an explosive odor is present. More intent, active but methodical sniffing behavior and tail wagging. I did not need to wait for the final response because she had convinced me with her behavior, so I recalled her. Upon investigation of the choke point, Explosive Ordinance Disposal (EOD) team members discovered an estimated 30 pounds of Homemade Explosive (HME) buried about 12 inches deep in the choke point.

In that moment it was a sense of complete validation. All the hard work, long hours, countless trials and training sessions to get prepared for operations in a combat zone had paid off. That was the first of many finds for my SSD. She was the only reason I made it home to my family and I owe her my life. If you rewind time, from a training standpoint, it all started with a game of positive association, building a strong foundation and properly imprinting my dog on odor. There are only a select few people to whom I attribute any success I've had in the MWD Program and Paul Bunker is one of them. He had a tremendous impact on me by deepening my understanding of behavior modification, odor work and operant conditioning. Paul is very accomplished and well known as a true subject matter expert in the K-9 community and I am fortunate to have served with and trained alongside him.

I met Paul at the Department of Defense (DoD) MWD training center at Lackland Air Force Base in 2006 when I had been K-9 for 6 years. At that point Paul had already completed a 22-year career in the British military where he served in various roles in their K-9 Program. After retirement, he helped establish the SSD program for the Army at Ft Leonard Wood, MO and then transferred to Lackland to help get our DoD SSD Program on the right track. He brought a wealth of expertise, operational and training experience and a passion for training dogs and handlers....but mainly the dogs. Paul's positive and almost immediate impact on the SSD Course cannot be understated, especially given the importance of our mission during the global war on terrorism. He developed a training plan that was effective and efficient to ensure we met our ultimate mission of sending well-trained dog teams overseas.

Key portions of my foundation for detection were developed during my years working with Paul, which would benefit countless Marines over the remainder of my career. I was able to develop my Marines into better trainers because Paul had developed me into a better trainer. This book provides techniques which will greatly contribute to your success as a dog trainer, regardless of your discipline. Paul's systematic approach to training is proven, effective and developed over years of lessons learned. I'm proud to know you, brother.

K-9 Leads the Way!
Chris Willingham
Master Sergeant (RET), United States Marine Corps
President, United States War Dog Association

BACKGROUND

Many years ago, I joined an off-leash detection dog program as the Senior Technical Advisor. It was an extended program of training lasting over three months, and ultimately the dogs would complete a two-week assessment at an operationally realistic location. Each handler was assigned two green (untrained) dogs, which they trained throughout the course in various tasks. Not long after taking on the role I became very frustrated as I watched dogs go through the final operational assessment phase at the very end of the course clearly not meeting the standards to graduate. Many weeks had been invested in training, but right at the end, they were not ready. The end goal was that each handler left the course with one operational dog. I realized if we waited to intervene until the last phase of training, we had wasted an opportunity to make meaningful and more effective changes earlier in the program. I instigated a system of essential skills assessments (progress checks) and made changes to the training program. This meant each dog had to pass milestones (progress checks) to continue on the training program. If it did not meet standard at each progress check the dog would be allowed five days additional training and retry. Failure to meet standard on the second attempt would move the dog back two weeks to a team in a follow-on class. This provided the dog extra training to meet the standard but also meant that the remaining dog had more time invested into its training and therefore even better at the final phase.

Firstly, I changed the existing training approach to adjust how the dogs were trained in systems of search. The dogs were trained by placing a target odor out and letting the dogs work until they found the target odor. This resulted in what I termed "wild dogs" as they learned to run around until they happened upon the target odor. As long as they responded they would be rewarded, further compounding the issue. The school had a methodology that every time a dog responded on odor, it MUST be rewarded, regardless if it was the consequence of incorrect behavior. So, if a dog ran wild, ignoring any cues (commands) from its handler and found the target odor, it would still be rewarded. I stopped this practice and instigated a six-week control phase where dogs had to learn the systems of search through positive reinforcement and without using the odor. Once the dogs had passed progress checks on obedience and directional cues, they progressed to imprinting. This made a massive difference to the dogs' standards in directional control and systems of search as it was taught independent of the target odor.

Next, I formalized the progress checks and integrated them throughout the training program. If a dog did not pass an assessment, it received five days of remedial training and would try again. If it still didn't pass, it was moved back to the training course one month behind and allowed to redo the prior months' training. Thus, dogs only progressed to the operational assessment phase if they demonstrated proficiency with the skills and behaviors that would enable them to pass the assessment. This proved highly effective, and a robust management approach with defined standards criteria meant the dogs progressed at their pace, but the course stayed on schedule.

INTRODUCTION

Thank you for purchasing this book. I look forward to guiding you through my system of imprinting detection dogs, and I hope you find the information here accessible and helpful.

This workbook aims to guide you through the proven steps I use to train a green (a term for untrained) detection dog to detect and respond to a target odor over the course of 15 days. I will teach you how to handle and store your training aids effectively and even how to systematically record your training sessions to keep track of your progression. By the time you have completed the steps in this workbook, I hope you will better understand imprinting and continue your journey in training your detection dog.

If you follow the progressive steps outlined in this workbook, you will shape a dog with little to no detection skills into one that is trained in a target odor's imprinting process. Even if your dog has had some training, the progressive steps I utilize allow you the flexibility to start the dog on the program and still be successful. The program is based on positive reinforcement; a reward-based training plan. It may be a good idea to read through the contents of the book, making notes as you read through, and then get all of the required equipment together. Then you will be prepared to begin following the progressive steps outlined in the book. Some of the steps can be practiced concurrently with other steps as you take the path to the end goal. There is a flowchart with a visual step-by-step approach for you to follow. When using the visual approach, do ensure you follow the flowchart and the correct sequence in which to train the dog(s). Complete the exercises (per the criteria) and ensure you record all training on the appropriate progress check. Using this systematic approach to the training, you will develop the skills necessary to complete the objectives of imprinting your dog on a target odor.

A word of caution: not all dogs are suited to detection work, as much as we desire them to possess the capability. Consider that some dogs do have physical restrictions, and some simply lack the desire. Each step in this workbook concludes with a progress check. These milestone events must be achieved to move forward and, as each is sequential, must be completed in the workbook's order. If your dog cannot reach the required progress check, there is no point moving forward as you will compound the issue and cause stress resulting in inadequate training. If you hit a roadblock, take a break and adjust training to suit the dog's learning level.

Imprinting is one small, albeit critical, part of a detection dogs' repertoire and the aim of this workbook is to give you a starting point to train dogs in detection. You may wish to go no further than imprint your dog and use the process to add enrichment to the dog's life. In which case this workbook provides you the steps to complete the process and use the skills learned to provide the dog, and yourself, an interesting hobby and method of enrichment. The simple process of teaching scent work stimulates learning and can help with a dog's mental welfare (Duranton & Horowitz, 2019). However, if you are interested in pursuing a formal application of the imprinting into detection then this first stage will provide you a clear indication if the dog is capable of continuing into the field. Without the ability to detect and respond on a target odor the dog would not be able to continue into more advanced training required in detection.

Is this the only way to imprint a detection dog? Absolutely not! Is it the only way that I personally imprint a detection dog? Absolutely not! But what I include in this book is the easiest and most broadly effective way. It is a method that can be used by following a progression plan, and as long as you stick to the plan, it will assist you to imprint your dog. It's also a method used by a range of people with different goals; conservation, environmental, leaks, spills, narcotics, weapons, and the list goes on. The approach in this book doesn't require fancy gear, only some containers for the imprinting phase, which can be simple glass jars. No need for scent boxes, odor carousels, remote reward delivery devices, or odor walls.

What this workbook is not going to teach you is the science behind the training. The workbook is a step-by-step progression to enable you to reach an end goal. It is developed from techniques I have used over the decades and the system I utilize to imprint dogs on a target odor. There will be no links to long scientific papers or citations from quotes related to the concepts. I do include some references to my related works to provide you with background information. If you want to learn about odor or animal learning, of course there are a plethora of books dedicated to those subjects and these books would go into greater depth than possible or necessary for the concepts in this workbook.

I read a book by James Clear called Atomic Habits, which discusses the importance of making small improvements, over time, to make enhancements in all that you do. While James was talking about people and their habits, it applies just as well to your dog training program. I will post his video about the 1% Rule on the workbook resources page. By taking the time to carefully source and select your target odors, handle and store them correctly, and prevent contamination (of your training odor and the environment), you will improve the quality of your training and detection standards.

Welfare

The dog's general welfare is paramount. Feeding, living arrangements, socialization, and enrichment time are critical facets of welfare for a dog. The 1% Rule applies to all these aspects of its life and more. In the context of this workbook, I will talk specifically about how the dog's welfare is related to learning. First and foremost, the dog must be comfortable in its working environment. While it is essential to follow the progression plans in sequence, there is no point trying to press on if the dog is stressed and/or demonstrating displacement behaviors. If the dog is not invested in the learning, take a break and allow the dog to stretch its legs and decompress. Then start again but take smaller steps and build it up. When the dog needs them, these breaks will pay dividends and, in the long run, keep the training on track. If you push a dog that's just not feeling it, you will taint the training session, the training environment, and potentially the whole process. If the dog is confused or stressed, it will demonstrate displacement behaviors (see terminology); you should be aware of the dog's body language and stop the session.

I have a bowl of water available during all training sessions. If the dog needs a drink, I don't stop it. Eating a bunch of cheese and chicken can dry the mouth out and make the dog thirsty, so having a drink is not an issue.

When you think about it, fifteen days is not a long time to invest some focused effort into training. Still, this amount of time is actually proven to be sufficient to take an average dog from knowing nothing about detection to imprinted on its first odor. However, learning must be at the dog's pace! Fifteen days is an achievable goal to imprint a dog, but if you take 16, 17, or even longer because that's the pace of your dog, that is perfectly fine.

Finally, I am English by birth. I was educated in England, spent most of my life in England, and speak with an English accent. I now live in the U.S., mostly Texas, and I have attempted to write this book in Standard American English. So, I accept there may be terms, spelling, or grammar which appear incorrect. At the same time, I have attempted to be as accurate as possible; please accept that American is my second language. If you are English reading this: Yes, they do spell things differently in the U.S.!

So, let's start the journey.

Terminology

There are a variety of terms used in the dog world and they are hardly universal. For instance, conditioning a dog to a clicker can be termed bridging, imprinting, or charging (plus others). Imprinting, within the context of this workbook, is the term used to condition a dog to respond to a target odor. Additionally, some people use the term *reinforcer* and some use *reward*. For this workbook, I will use reward as the standard term for a reinforcer. To assist you in understanding the terminology used within this workbook, a glossary is included below.

Blank	A container identical to your target container but which has no added odor or items.
Bribe	A bribe is showing the dog a reward to influence a behavior.
Bridge the click	The method of building an association between a marker and a reward. Also known as bridging the clicker, charging the click(er), and imprinting the clicker.
Clicker	Typically, a small plastic box with a metal strip that, when depressed and released, makes a "tik-tok" sound.
Displacement behaviors	A behavior demonstrated by a dog when it is confused or stressed. It can be scratching, lip licking, sniffing the ground, or any behavior out-of-context.
Directional cues	A term to describe the system used to guide a dog through a survey area by communicating that the dog should move to the left, right, away, or towards the handler while searching.
Extinction	When a behavior is not reinforced with a reward it will decrease.
Grey behaviors	A confused type of behavior when the dog is unclear precisely what is expected, so performs what it "thinks" is correct, but it is not.
Imprint	The process of teaching a dog a target odor.
Interferent	An odor (or item) that is used as a distraction during imprinting and is not a target scent.
Marker	Typically, a sound that communicates to the dog it has reached the criteria of behavior, and a reinforcer (reward) is coming.
Odor Recognition Test (ORT)	A standardized system to evaluate a dog's capability to detect and respond to a target odor while ignoring interferents. The majority of certification organizations utilize them.
Progress check	A milestone gatepost which the dog must pass to continue through the progression plan.
Progression plan	A systematic approach to training behaviors in a written plan.
Proof/ing	Proofing is the technique of practicing a behavior in different situations and environments to enable the dog to generalize the behavior in various scenarios.
Reinforcer	Something that strengthens a behavior. (see reward)

Reward	A reinforcer that the dog finds pleasurable. (see reinforcer)
Scent cone	The movement of odor molecules from the target source when there is an air current. A scent cone is formed moving downwind of the source.
Scent container	The container used specifically for odor training. This container is placed within a training area used for your dog to search and contains either target or interferent odor or is blank.
Scent plume	See Scent cone.
Scent pool	A pool of scent that forms around a target odor when there is no air movement.
Target odor	An odor that has been identified as a scent which the dog must find and respond to.
Variable reward	A system I utilize to provide the dog "a reward" for each successful completion of behavior; however, the dog never knows "what" the reward is. Sometimes a treat, or praise, or a ball, for instance.

CHAPTER 1 – HOW TO USE THIS BOOK

"If you can't explain it to a six-year-old, you don't understand it yourself."
— Albert Einstein

The book is separated into stand-alone chapters. Each chapter details a specific topic in the imprinting process. While chapters in this workbook such as clicker training, storage and handling, or even reward selection may be "old hat" to you, I would suggest it's worth reading to follow my methodology. You never know; you may learn something you feel can be part of your program.

One of the aims I had when writing this workbook was to make it accessible and affordable. To me, there is no reason to write a book with the intent to help people, then add a considerable purchase price to it. So to cut costs and make it accessible to as many people as possible, I had to make some sacrifices. For instance, I would have liked to have colored tabs so you can quickly go from chapter to chapter when picking up the book. But the cost was prohibitive, and you can buy colored tabs for about $1 and add them yourself. Also, I decided not to include a lot of photographs as they push the price up considerably. There are diagrams when needed to illustrate a concept, but not images. However, I have created a resources page within my website to support the workbook, including resources such as videos and photographs to help you further understand a concept.

The resources page will be updated as time goes on, so keep checking back and making sure you get the latest advice and guidance. Each chapter with a practical training element will be supported through media files including videos. These resources support learning by providing visual examples of the techniques discussed. The page can be found at:

www.Chiron-K9.com/imprinting-book

For those chapters that are training-focused, there are Progression Plans included. These Progression Plans guide you through each step in the training process. What they do not tell you is how you MUST train the step. I will offer my methods and guidance but, in the end, you will train the dog in front of you and must be able to adjust each step to suit your particular situation.

Train the Dog in Front of You

In 2020 I had a contract to train eight detection dogs for a research project. There were seven Pointers and a Labrador. All were adopted from a federal agency as they were not selected for the agency canine program. One of the Pointers, who happened to be my favorite dog, was very sensitive in training. He would show displacement behaviors if he was confused and panicked when he didn't understand the task. In his instance, I had to break the progression plan down into smaller steps than the other dogs, as he needed that extra level of training. But once I did, and I showed him what to do, he accelerated his pace of learning and then caught on much more quickly to the task. He was also a dog that had little-to-no interest in treats, so I had to use a ball for most of his training. While this typically means lower repetitions of training, it was fortunate that he enjoyed just holding a ball and being petted and praised. This is only one example of how each dog is an individual, and sometimes we have to adjust the training plan accordingly to meet the end goal. But that is fine! It's part of being a good trainer. You must be able to assess a dog and develop the training steps to meet the dog's needs and not just blindly follow a plan.

How This Book is Structured

The chapters are in sequence of the training plan, each building on the one before. It is possible to clicker train while you are sourcing your scent items, but you cannot imprint (with this system) before you have clicker trained. To help you visualize the process, I have added a roadmap of the system below.

This is a workbook, and I intended it to be used as such—pencil out sentences, paragraphs, or sections that do not work for you. Make notes in the margins and add your thoughts as you progress. Additionally, I have added notes sections at the end of each chapter for you to jot down anything you feel needs recorded.

In all my timelines, I have imprinting being 15 days in length. My criteria are that by the end of the 15 days, the dog will understand a target odor (just one) and respond to it using the desired response. Of course, dogs are living beings and not machines, and there will be those that complete this process in less time and those that need a little more time. There will also be those that never get to the end goal.

To help reach these defined criteria, I use Progress Checks, which involve assessing the dog against a set of standards and ensuring it reaches them before moving ahead. As the dog achieves each task criteria, it moves onto the next stage. If the dog does not meet the task criteria, it is reset to train the previous step and try again. Within this workbook, you will find progress checks as you move from one step to the next.

So, use the steps in this workbook, use the progress checks and be robust and critical in your assessments as this will benefit you and the dog in the end.

On the next page is a chart which provides a roadmap for you to follow. It shows you which tasks can be completed concurrently, and which are independent. Do not worry if some parts take longer; for instance, if you order your scent and it does not arrive before clicker training has finished. But you should not move on until the task prior has been completed within the roadmap.

At the end of each task, there is a progress check. This check should be completed following the criteria and the results recorded. It's a simple go/no-go criterion, no complicated math or formulas. Your dog can either reach the standard, or it cannot. I have included a section at the end of each training plan which you can use to record the results of the progress check or you can make your own.

The workbook is designed to be opened at the page you are working on and laid flat on a surface so you can see the steps without having to keep opening or pages flipping over. Below is a sample training plan, including overview, steps for success, and progression plan. While some of the areas are obvious by their title, I strongly recommend you read through the training plan, from start to finish, before commencing that lesson with your dog.

Roadmap

TASK	DAY 1	2	3	4	5	6	7	8	9	10	11	12	13	14	15
Procure Odor															
Establish Storage															
Reward Selection Assessment	Lesson 1 & 2														
Clicker Training		Lesson 3	Lesson 3	Lesson 4											
Lure the Sit			Lesson 5	Lesson 6											
Response Training					Lesson 7	Lesson 7	Lesson 8	Lesson 9	Lesson 10						
Imprinting										Lesson 11	Lesson 12	Lesson 13	Lesson 14	Lesson 15	Lesson 16

Lesson Overview			
Event	This section describes the training event.	Day	1
		Lesson No.	1
Equipment	This section details the equipment required to conduct the training event.		
Location	This section describes the type of location to be utilized.		
Duration	This section provides guidance on the time duration the event should take.		
Aim	This section describes the aim of the event.		
Objectives	This section lists the training objectives to be achieved at the end of the training event.		
Prerequisite Lesson	This section details the prior lesson that must be completed before conducting this training.	Prerequisite Lesson No.	1
Setup	This section describes the setup of the training event.		

The day of the 15-day timeline

The prerequisite lesson number

Remarks
This section is for you to make any remarks or notes related to the training event for future lessons.

Quick Look
The QR code can be scanned on a mobile device and is linked to a short video demonstrating the lesson's concepts. The video is not the entire lesson.

Steps to Success	
Step	Action
The steps are sequential and must be completed in order.	This section describes, in detail, the steps necessary to carry out the training sessions that make up the progression plan.

Progression Plan			
Task No	Subtask Number	Description	Number of treats/clicks
This section provides the task number.	This section provides the subtask number.	This section provides a summary of the training carried out for each subtask.	This section details the number of repetitions to be completed.

Progress Check	
This section describes the behavioral criteria the dog must meet in order to progress to the next lesson.	Yes/No
This section details which training to repeat if the dog does not meet the criteria above.	

Equipment

Each training plan includes an equipment list detailing what you will need for that particular lesson. However, as this is a workbook aimed at teaching imprinting within a 15-day window of time, I feel it is important to set out an equipment list early in the process. That way, you have the opportunity to order (now) anything you'll need (later), so you won't have to pause your training while you wait for some piece of equipment to be delivered.

The specifics of what you will require depends on what you are using as a target odor, the resulting storage and handling requirements and what, if any, equipment you already own. As a guide, below is a list of suggested items specific to the imprinting.

- CLICKER – Any type of clicker is fine, or any marker you want to use.
- KONG – This is to be cut up for odor and separate from the KONG you reward your dog with (if applicable).
- PILL BOTTLE LID – Or something similar, could be a plastic cap from a sports drink or even from a plastic milk bottle.
- TREATS – A mix of commercial and fresh (cheese, sandwich meat, etc.).
- DISPOSABLE GLOVES – Discussed in detail in the storage and handling chapter.
- STORAGE CONTAINERS – Includes mason jars, large medical pots, Ziplock bags, and ammunition cans.
- IMPRINT (scent) CONTAINERS – Could include Mason jars, spice shakers, glass saltshakers, and Training Aid Detection Devices (TADDs).
    o You can purchase food-grade stainless steel spice shakers with a wire gauze or lid with holes online for a few dollars each and these work perfectly. I also have used Mason jars with an additional wire gauze instead of the metal screw lid they come with, as well as made holes in the lid.
    o The Training Aid Delivery Device™ (TADD) was explicitly designed to support canine detection training and work. They can be purchased in 2 oz, 4oz, 8oz, and 12oz sizes and made of glass or plastic. The jars are designed as a safe sample containment system while allowing target odor molecules to be released from a special membrane. The TADD can contain liquid, small particles, and hazardous material, and it has been utilized on COVID-19 Detection Dog trials. The lid includes a gas-tight chemical-resistant gasket, which holds a hydrophobic and oleophobic membrane. There is also a safety grid to protect the membrane and the contents from the dog. TADD's and stainless-steel shakers are available from Scientific Canine Solutions™ (SciK9) website (www.scik9.com).

CHAPTER 2 – REWARD SELECTION

In this chapter, we start at the very beginning of the training process. Reward selection is one of the earliest assessments I conduct when starting a dog on a training program. This assessment is a short, easy-to-follow exercise that can be repeated as often as you like throughout the training process and beyond into maintenance training. I would encourage you to repeat it as part of your maintenance training program, just like doing obedience, directional, and search training. It's a great starter exercise if you take group training as it demonstrates each dog's individuality. As you conduct the assessment, you may realize that even your own dog has different favorite rewards than you initially thought. This exercise takes the guesswork out of that process and can enhance your training standards. Consider the principles of accelerated learning:

1. The reward is of high value.
2. The reward immediately follows the behavior.
3. Behavior is consistently rewarded.

More on the second and third principles later. We will tap into the first principle, "reward is of high value," for this chapter.

Why is Reward Selection Important?

Many years ago, when I started training dogs formally in the military, the instructor on my basic dog trainers' course told me that only bad (I am being kind with using that word compared to what he said to me) trainers use food to train dogs. Being the young eighteen-year-old soldier I was and wanting to be a great dog trainer, I took my Sergeant's advice and didn't use food. Back in those days, we never used toy rewards either. The training was hard. Now that I look back on it, we made it hard! About fifteen years later, the Mine Detection Dog project I spoke about earlier started, and that's when I began to use clickers and food treats for training. I then realized how much time I had wasted doing all that ask-tell-make-pull on the lead training.

All too often, people select rewards based on their personal preference. It's because they see other trainers using them, or they already have them from training other dogs, or maybe they believe it is rewarding for the dog and grab one off a pet store shelf. Whatever the reason, it can be the case that the dog hasn't had an opportunity to choose the reward it likes. The dog chases a ball, sure, but does it enjoy that solid rubber ball as much as, say, a KONG or a tennis ball? What if you gave the dog its favorite reward after an excellent behavior it just demonstrated? The accelerated learning principles tell us the dog is more likely to repeat the behavior if the reward is of high value to the dog. Therefore, by using its favorite reward for those times the dog demonstrates an excellent learned behavior, we are accelerating the learning. Isn't that precisely what we want to do in all our training?
The reward must be rewarding to the dog!

You can manipulate behavior through the correct application of the reward. A higher value reward will help accelerate learning and maintain the desire to work. In the same light, you can reduce motivation by using lower value rewards. Sometimes this is an advantage; for instance, when I was training at the US military's Lackland Air Force Base, home of the Department of Defense Military Working Dog School, we would get very high drive Malinois to train. If you tried to train these dogs with a red KONG, they would become over-aroused and not be stable enough to learn. Their drive would be so high they would exhibit what I call "red mist," an informal British term meaning losing control or impaired judgment—making training the dogs very difficult. So, I purchased cheap, heavy, solid rubber dog reward balls from a well-known U.S. chain store. These were not as high value to the Malinois, and we could keep them at an arousal level to allow training. They had sufficient drive to accept the ball as a reward, but it did not have enough value to send them over the edge.

Hierarchy of Rewards

The first stage in the reward selection process is to conduct an assessment to identify a reward the dog finds rewarding. The second stage is to build a hierarchy of rewards so you can use them effectively in both initial training and maintenance training.

I prefer my dogs accept both food and toys as rewards and so I conduct assessments for both types of rewards. However, do not forget that your voice and physical praise are just as, if not more rewarding. Regardless of if I am using a toy or food reward, I will also be praising and physically rewarding the dog. Sometimes I may just use praise, or physical reward, or both and also add in food, treats, or a toy. Do not be predictable in your reward schedule and use rewards to manipulate behavior.

Now I have spoken a lot about toys as rewards, but the food is just as rewarding! But just like toy rewards, we need to find out which food the dog finds rewarding. I tend to use cheese, chicken, bologna, sandwich meat, and small commercial reward treats. I still complete a reward selection process, but I often mix the treats into my bag, so the dog gets a surprise as to what is pulled out for a reward. However, I still get dogs that spit out some types of treats, so what's the point of offering them in training if the dogs don't like them? The treats are clearly not rewarding and therefore do not reinforce a behavior. Learning certainly is not accelerated in this case.

The aim is to achieve a hierarchy of rewards. We use the highest reward in the hierarchy as the "jackpot." The jackpot is reserved for the exceptional learning points, for those significant behaviors that made us smile on the inside and to reward the dog for a job well done. The next reward in the hierarchy is used for routine training daily. It is important to enable training to be balanced and reward the dog without over stimulating or satisfying all of its reward desire. The third in the hierarchy I will use more in maintenance type training. However, I will mix it up at times, so the dog just never knows what reward it will get. Unless it does something outstanding when it knows it will always get its favorite reward for a great job well done!

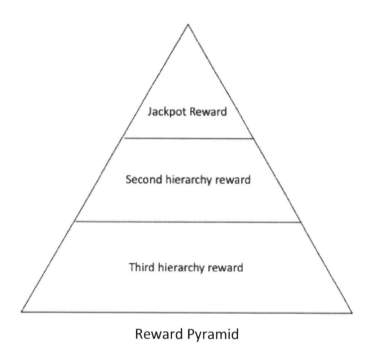

Reward Pyramid

Variable Reward Delivery

I like to use a system of variable reward delivery. The technique I use might be slightly different than the variable reward you are used to, but this works for me. Variable reward delivery starts during the imprinting phase and continues for the life of the dog. The main reason that I use variable reward delivery is that during environmental and conservation work, the dog may have many finds during a single day. As an example, my dog and I once had 183 confirmed finds in one day! You can imagine rewarding the dog with its toy 183 times. The poor thing would be tired, and reward satisfied after the eighth find.

For this reason, I reward the dog every time it has a find, but I vary the reward. Sometimes it's a toy, a treat, or praise. But the dog always gets something. Using this system means I can use treats, and the dog doesn't get tired by playing with the reward. It also means the reward disappears quickly and we are back to work. Once in a while, the dog will get a toy, but it doesn't know which toy it will get. The second or third in the hierarchy comes out more often than the first "jackpot" reward, which is saved for an excellent job and used sparingly. The advantage for imprinting is that I can conduct many repetitions of the training session using treats. The dog will keep going without being fatigued, or its reward drives satisfied. We have completed 40 trials in succession during some research trials without issue, and the dogs maintain the same detection and response standards. It also means that if I am in a situation where rewarding the dog would put it into danger by chasing a reward, I can provide a treat or physical/verbal praise, and the dog does not get frustrated or confused.

Why is Variable Reward Effective?

When I was conducting the development of the Mine Detection Dog project, there was a dilemma of rewarding the dog during operational searches. The requirement was that the dog detected and indicated three mines in a lane of 50 meters x 1 meter and reached the casualty within a set period of time. My recollection is that period of time is about 50 minutes. Before this project, I was taught that you had to reward a dog every time it detected a target; if you didn't, it would lose interest and not respond to the next detection target. So, by that reckoning, if the team searches a lane and locates a mine but the dog is not rewarded, then the dog will not respond on the next mine it encounters during the same search. Of course, this was not acceptable and a concern. I decided to reward the dogs with a treat and not the usual tennis ball as my thinking was that a treat reward is safer than a ball reward in a minefield. It makes sense! When we first tried the technique, what I observed confused me because it contradicted the training approach that I was taught for the previous fifteen years. Rather than reducing the dogs' drive, receiving a treat and not the ball actually increased it. When they went back to work, I could see the dogs get more intense in their search behavior and hear their sniffing behavior. The dogs continued to work even more challenging tasks after the second target was located and still responded on the third, at which point they were rewarded with a tennis ball, which was their jackpot toy.

As it happened, there was a Regimental Dinner (formal military event) the weekend after I tried this new system out, and I was seated next to a former Sergeant Major called Alec Coull (Alec will pop up again in this book). Alec was a dog trainer before his time, and while a tough former Scottish infantryman, he was a great character that would talk dogs all night. But not just "in my day dogs had 78 teeth" type talk—I mean deep training conversations that I loved. So, I told him about my experience, and he just smiled and said, "partial reward!" He then went on to explain the concept in simple terms and why it works.

A note here: do not confuse the terms I use in this book with the terminology used in other areas of training. Some people use the term partial reward, or intermittent reward, when talking about NOT rewarding the dog on every correct execution of behavior (or even a click/mark). In this case, I am using partial reward, as that was Alec's term, to describe rewarding every successful behavior but with different levels of value of the reward.

I will now try my best to articulate the Alec Coull meaning of partial reward, bearing in mind that I am neither Scottish nor full of whiskey at this time.

Imagine you walk into a bar; you have $1.00, and you want a beer. You see a fruit machine (translation: slot machine) in the corner and the lights are flashing, it is playing theme music from an old 1980's movie. Knowing that it is a way for you to get what you want (enough money for a beer) and provide the jackpot you wander over. Looking at the reels, you see they are lined up as:

Lemon, Melon, Melon, Melon.

If only the three melons are held and the first reel drops a melon, you could buy fifty beers with that win! So, you put your money in, and the reels don't hold, of course, but you could still win. You press the start button, and off the reels go. Dropping in one at a time:

Melon, Lemon, Cherry, Star.

So close, a little disappointing, but you still have a chance. Spin again:

Cherry, Cherry, Cherry, Melon.

Great that's $0.50 you won, so you are back to a dollar. Not entirely what you want, but it's something, AND on the row above the winning line, there is:

Melon, Lemon, Melon, Melon.

And on the row below the winning line it's:

Cherry, Melon, Star, Lemon.

Now, if only those four melons dropped in. It is very close, and you already got something, so you spin again:

Melon, Cherry, Melon, Lemon.

Spin again:

Lemon, Cherry Melon, Melon.

So close. Spin again:

Cherry, Cherry, Cherry, Lemon.

$0.50 again. But you keep feeling the jackpot is just in the next try so you spin and get nothing. The jackpot must be in the next try, spin, nothing, spin, nothing, and your money is gone. Fruit machines use the partial reward system, and they work because they give smaller rewards with the "promise" that the jackpot is coming; just try one more time. Of course, the fruit machine always wins in the long run, although you hear the ching, ching, and ching noise of a winner every so often. This is what we are doing with the dogs with a system of variable reward delivery; we are giving them cherries and saying try again, the jackpot is out there, so they try harder, get a cherry but know the jackpot is out there. Then, once in a while, they get that jackpot, and all the effort was worth it.

Reward Selection—Toys

The reward selection assessment is straightforward and should only take 15 minutes per session, 1 hour total. Once the dog understands the game, it will take even less time depending on how long you spend playing with the dog once it has selected its reward (for toys).

Firstly, we need to select a variety of rewards: KONG, rubber ball, tennis ball, rope tug, and ball on a rope, for instance.

Toy selection will be based on some factors that you need to consider:

> Is the toy safe for the dog?
> Is it convenient for your training?
> Is it replaceable?
> Is it affordable?
> Your interaction level – Do YOU enjoy the reward?

Is the toy safe for the dog?

We need to consider safety, not just in terms of the toy's construction but also concerning its size. You should not choose a tennis ball for a possessive Malinois, for instance. The dog will clamp down on that ball, burst it and then hold on to the remains like it's a long-lost bone, but more importantly, there is a risk the dog will swallow it.

Is it convenient for your training?

When I started handling an Oil Detection Canine, my dog (Kaye) was a large 90lb female black Labrador who loved a KONG rubber ball. It was her favorite reward, so on her first deployment to a spill on a river in Canada, I thought I would use her "jackpot" toy as I transferred her from training real-life searches (more on the transfer later). For her first-ever find in the field, I wanted to jackpot reward her and was so excited when I saw her change in behavior as she followed a scent cone to the source. When I saw Kaye was at the source, I threw the ball and gave out a cheer of delight. Of course, Kaye had been conditioned to give a sit response at the source and was not expecting to hear me cheer, let alone for a rubber ball to come bouncing by as she turned to see what all the commotion was about. The ball hit the source perfectly, but it continued to roll on, being a KONG rubber ball with plenty of bounce. Unfortunately, we were on the sloping side of a riverbank, and before Kaye could grab the ball, it rolled into the water and quickly out of sight. That's the last time we saw that ball, and Kaye was mighty annoyed with me! From that day on, I selected rewards that were convenient to the training as it was not acceptable that every time a dog finds a source of the target, it loses its reward. In this case, Kaye and I compromised, and she would get an orange floating KONG or a large tennis ball on river searches!

Is it replaceable?

We want the dog to receive the reward it enjoys, but this can have limitations. If the reward isn't easily replaced, then losing it can be a real issue. The reward selection assessment needs to utilize rewards that can be sourced without too much trouble.

I was once training a Golden Retriever for detection and he LOVED his blue and white marbled KONG - not sure if they make them anymore as I have never seen one since. However, one day I didn't have that KONG on me, and I rewarded him with the classic red one. He initially went after the reward, briefly mouthed it, then went straight back to responding on the source. I felt so bad for him as he was waiting for his favorite reward, and I didn't have it. I don't think they even make that same type of KONG now, and it was replaced with the pink puppy version. So learn from my mistakes and don't train with a one-of-a-kind reward!

Is it affordable?

Unless you can afford to replace the rewards often, you need something durable, play resistant, and not too expensive. I love KONG toys for this very reason, and generally, I find dogs enjoy them. They have such a variety of designs, sizes, and types that you can find something to suit most dogs.

Your interaction level – Do YOU enjoy the reward?

The reward is just one part of the rewarding process. Reward time should not consist solely of a "reward dispenser" (that's you). Your participation in the rewarding process will likely be just as meaningful to the dog as the reward itself. So, if you have a bias towards a particular toy, for instance, then you will put more effort into the reward stage and make the toy more rewarding through your actions. But don't be false with your reward behavior; if you have a bias, then accept it and continue as naturally as possible. Because you cannot maintain a false level of motivation for a particular reward forever, trying to fake it will be detrimental to training in the longer term. We need to balance the reward being enjoyable for the dog and your interactions with the rewarding process. Just be yourself and allow the dog to learn how the toy interacts with the both of you.

Making Good Use of the Reward

The reward is NOT a bribe. If you have to continually show the dog you have a reward to get it to complete a behavior, you have bribed it. That is not good training since the reward is then a cue to conduct a behavior and not a consequence for a behavior. You will use luring in part of this training program, but it is faded fast so it is the behavior that becomes rewarding. Luring is an excellent training technique to establish a concept in the dog's mind but must be stopped as soon as possible and make the behavior an act that is rewarded, not one that's bribed. If you do have to show your dog a reward to get it to do something, all is not lost. It is not difficult to reprogram the dog's mind from bribery to reward.

There is no point in having a reward, especially one the dog loves, and not using it. Seems a strange statement to make, right? I have seen people reward their dogs with a toy and the dog returns to the handler proud and happy, only to have the toy pulled out of its mouth and shoved back into a pocket. I have seen that more than once, and that's too often! The reward isn't just the toy or even the treat; it's the rest of the reward play stage. It's the interaction, verbal praise, petting and stroking, throwing for a retrieve. It's the understanding that payday is payday, but the reward of a toy and/or treat and the effort that the handler puts into communicates how pleased they are. When you reward your dog, make sure it knows that this is the best thing that's happened!

Conducting Reward Assessments

This assessment can be conducted by just one person; an assistant is always helpful but not required.

I like to conduct the assessment in a room with minimal distractions so the dog can focus on the exercise. You can use any room where the dog isn't distracted by other people, animals, or anything else they find attractive. Remember, we are conducting an assessment to start training, and in some cases, the dog has to learn the game before we get the results we want. We are not trying to assess the dog's environmental soundness; we are focused on its reward selection only.

The first step is to ensure your dog understands the reward. By this, I mean you have to interact with the dog and ensure the dog realizes exactly what the reward has to offer. The dog should not experience the reward for first time during the assessment.

Making reward time interactive between you and your dog is important, so take your dog out and have some fun with the toys you're going to use during the assessment. Play fetch, play tug, and allow the dog to chase the reward and understand what it's worth. Remember, you need a selection of at least five toys and preferably focused on the type of play your dog enjoys. If it's a dog that enjoys chase and fetch, use KONG, tennis ball, rubber ball, squeaky ball, etc. If it's a tug drive dog, use KONG on a rope, rope, or ball on a rope, etc.

There are two assessments: toy and food. You can complete the assessment that suits your training plan or, if, like me, you use both types of reward, then complete them both.

Accelerate Learning with a Hierarchy of Rewards

By ensuring you select rewards the dog enjoys, you are tapping into the potential power of a reward-based training system. It is not enough to just grab a toy and throw it in your basket at the local store. Make sure you put as much effort into preparation as you do the actual imprinting. Every 1% helps, and reward selection is worth way more than 1%.

Do not complete the assessment once and forget it. Repeat the assessment monthly as part of your maintenance training program. It is not unusual for a dog to change its mind and move the hierarchy of rewards around a bit. Also, change the rewards used in the selection by replacing the two rewards not chosen for new ones.

Remember, you can manipulate behavior through the use of the hierarchy of rewards. Either you are calming your dog or increasing motivation.

Training Plan, Lesson 1

Lesson Overview			
Event	Toy Reward Selection Assessment	Day	1
		Lesson No.	1
Equipment	At least 5 rewards the dog has played with previously		
Location	Indoor room with minimal distractions		
Duration	4 x 10 minutes		
Aim	To assess the dog's hierarchy of toy rewards		
Objectives	To conduct a toy reward selection assessment To assess the dog's hierarchy of rewards To establish a list of the dog's hierarchy of rewards		
Prerequisite Lesson	Nil	Prerequisite Lesson No.	
Setup	The dog should not be in the room while the assessment is set up. Have 5 preselected rewards that the dog has played with. Place the 5 rewards on the floor in a loose pile. Ensure no rewards are moving (a ball rolling around, for instance). After each selection event, the remove the chosen reward from the pile. Repeat the assessment to establish the hierarchy list for rewards.		
Remarks			
Note: There is a free webinar demonstrating concepts within this lesson on the workbook media page: www.Chiron-K9.com/imprinting-book			

Training Plan, Lesson 1 (pg. 2)

	Steps to Success
Step	**Action**
1	The dog is kept outside the room or in a kennel.
2	Place the 5 toys on the ground.
3	Bring the dog into the area of the toys and ensure it can see them.
4	Allow the dog, off-leash, to go to toys.
5	When it has selected a toy, leave the room with the dog and take the toy (do not play with the toy at this stage).
6	Record the toy it chose on the assessment form.
7	Place the toy back into the pile but move the items around, so they are not in the same pattern.
8	Repeat the process two more times, recording the dog's choice under "Toy Chosen."
9	The toy the dog chose the most is the "jackpot" reward. Remove it from the pile.
10	Repeat the assessment with the 4 remaining rewards.
11	You now have the secondary toy reward in the hierarchy list. Remove it from the pile.
12	Repeat the assessment with the 3 remaining rewards—you now have the third toy reward in the hierarchy list.

Toy Reward Assessment Record

	Toy chosen	Toy chosen the most
Assessment 1		
Trial 1		
Trial 2		
Trial 3		
Assessment 2		
Trial 1		
Trial 2		
Trial 3		
Assessment 3		
Trial 1		
Trial 2		
Trial 3		

Training Plan, Lesson 2

Lesson Overview			
Event	Treat Reward Selection Assessment	Day	1
		Lesson No.	2
Equipment	8 types of food reward which the dog has experienced previously		
Location	Indoor room with minimal distractions		
Duration	4 x 10 minutes		
Aim	To assess the dog's hierarchy of treat rewards		
Objectives	To conduct a treat reward selection assessment To assess the dog's hierarchy of treat rewards To establish a list of the dog's hierarchy of treat rewards		
Prerequisite Lesson	Toy Reward Selection Assessment – if applicable	Prerequisite Lesson No.	1
Setup	Have a variety of treats in different containers, one type of treat per container. Place the containers on a table within reach of a chair. Have hand wipes available to clean your hands between each session.		
Remarks			
Note: Additional blank forms are available to download on the workbook media page: www.Chiron-K9.com/imprinting-book			

Training Plan, Lesson 2 (pg. 2)

Once you have selected the treats you'll use for the assessment, offer the dog examples of each treat and allow it to taste them. Hold the treat in a loosely closed palm and will enable the dog to smell the treat in your hand before presenting it. Now that the dog has been exposed to the treats and understands their value, it's time to complete the assessment.

\multicolumn{2}{c}{Steps to Success}	
Step	Action
1	Select up to 8 different treats you wish to use for training.
2	Clean your hands with the wipes.
3	Hold a different treat loosely in each hand and allow the dog to smell them.
4	Whichever hand the dog pays more interest in, open the palm and let it get the treat.
5	Repeat this 2 more times, holding the same treats in the same hand.
6	The treat the dog pays more attention to is the treat you record in the record.
7	Repeat this process with different treats.
8	Record the favorite treat each time you complete an assessment.
9	You will be left with 1 treat by the end and a hierarchy of treats.

Training Plan, Lesson 2: Example of completed Treat Assessment Record

In this example:

	Treat 1	Treat 2
Assessment 1	Bacon	Liver
Assessment 2	Turkey	Chicken
Assessment 3	Cheese	Salami
Assessment 4	Bologna	Steak

	Treat chosen
Assessment 1	
Trial 1	Bacon
Trial 2	Bacon
Trial 3	Bacon

Bacon

	Treat chosen
Assessment 2	
Trial 1	Turkey
Trial 2	Chicken
Trial 3	Chicken

Chicken

	Treat chosen
Assessment 3	
Trial 1	Cheese
Trial 2	Cheese
Trial 3	Cheese

Cheese

	Treat chosen
Assessment 4	
Trial 1	Bologna
Trial 2	Steak
Trial 3	Bologna

Bologna

Bacon
Chicken
Bacon

Bacon

Cheese
Cheese
Cheese

Cheese

Bacon
Bacon
Bacon

Bacon

Hierarchy	Treat
1st	Bacon
2nd	Cheese
3rd	Bologna, Chicken

If you wish, you can assess the two third-place treats. However, I find that once you are at this level, the dog will take anything as a choice.

Training Plan, Lesson 2: Treat Assessment Record

This form is used to record the two treats you use in each trial.

	Treat 1	Treat 2
Assessment 1		
Assessment 2		
Assessment 3		
Assessment 4		

	Treat chosen
Assessment 1	
Trial 1	
Trial 2	
Trial 3	

	Treat chosen
Assessment 2	
Trial 1	
Trial 2	
Trial 3	

	Treat chosen
Assessment 3	
Trial 1	
Trial 2	
Trial 3	

	Treat chosen
Assessment 4	
Trial 1	
Trial 2	
Trial 3	

Hierarchy	Treat
1st	
2nd	
3rd	

NOTES

CHAPTER 3 – CLICKER TRAINING

"The way positive reinforcement is carried out is more important than the amount."
- B. F. Skinner

Firstly, I will clarify the terms "clicker" and "click" used in this workbook. You can replace the term clicker with any marker you wish to use; a whistle, beep sound, verbal "yes" cue, or anything else. It doesn't matter, in the context of this workbook, what you use as long as you are consistent. But for the sake of continuity, I will, from this point onwards, call it a clicker, so if you use something else, then either go through the workbook crossing out the words "click" and "clicker" and replace them with your marker or just read them as your marker.

Secondly, there are various terms for conditioning the dog to a clicker: imprinting, charging, bridging, conditioning, plus others, I am sure. In this workbook, the standardized term will be bridge and bridging.

What is Clicker Training?

I believe, but cannot assume, that most people reading this book will know what clicker training is. So, this chapter will be a revision for some but may be of interest to all. There are fantastic resources available elsewhere to teach clicker training; in this workbook, I will provide sufficient guidance to imprint your dog. But do not let your learning stop after this chapter. Continue to practice during training and beyond. I encourage you to take opportunities to expand your knowledge whenever possible.

As with a lot of dog training, there are variations within clicker training. The way I start bridging the clicker may not be the same as other people, courses, or training methods. They are not wrong, and I am not wrong. These are just variations on a theme that get to the same final result. I will describe how I bridge the clicker, and you can use that method, or use your current process (if you already have one that works), or you may decide to try a completely different approach. As long as the dog is conditioned to the click, it doesn't matter.

Clicker training, in basic terms, is bridging the sound of a clicker to a reinforcer. As described in the glossary, the clicker is typically a small plastic box, but can also be a phone app, a food jar lid, or even a pen flashlight for a blind dog. The click sound emitted from the device is bridged to a reward, and the dog is conditioned to understand that the "click" means a treat or toy is coming. The "click" marks the desired behavior, and the dog soon learns that repeating a behavior results in a "click" which then results in a reward.

In fact, I typically clicker train all the dogs I am training. Even if the clicker does not feature again in the training plan, I do this for several reasons:

- To build relationships and trust in the training.

- To condition the dog to learn.
- To build learning experiences of shaping, luring, and capture.
- To give me a tool that is already bridged if needed.
- To assist in training a handler – yes, really.

To Build Relationships and Trust in the Training

I have often trained dogs not knowing the background of the dog. They have come from vendors in Europe or rescue centers, and there is no way of knowing what their development or prior training experience was. Generally, these dogs do not know the clicker, and therefore, while the process is new, it is very rewarding and easy to learn. I find that even the most stressed dogs can become calmer during training once we engage in clicker training (it's that 1% Rule again). Building that trust and relationship at the start will get the dog into a learning mindset and help it relax during the training experience.

To Condition the Dog to Learn

I like to prepare the dog's mind to learn. Clicker training is a great way to do that. Once the dog understands the clicker training concept, it will be in charge of using its behaviors to make the clicks happen. By giving the dog this control and ability, they become invested in the learning process.

To Build Learning Experiences of Shaping, Luring, and Capture

Clicker training helps get the dog's brain ready to learn. Depending on where the dog came from, it may not understand that learning happens and can be manipulated by its behavior. I want the dog to understand it has an investment in the learning process, and if it actively gets involved it will earn great rewards, and plenty of them. I also want the dog to understand the different concepts of learning and how they work. That way, the dog knows the "game" we are playing and how to manipulate its behavior to win and get the reward.
I like to teach three learning strategies with the clicker once the dog is bridged:

- Lure – I typically use this to teach the sit or down depending on what the dog already knows, if anything. These are straightforward behaviors to teach.
- Capture – With capture, we are trying to mark a behavior the dog chooses to do naturally, encouraging it to then repeat the behavior.
- Shape – Shaping is the approximation of behaviors towards a final goal. For this, I usually teach the touch stick.

If the dog has learned a behavior using each of these strategies and the clicker, I find it understands the concept and how its behaviors can manipulate the click.

To Give Me a Tool that is Already Bridged if Needed

When the clicker is bridged at the start of a training program, then the tool is available at any time it is needed. This is so much easier than realizing you could do with a marker to develop behavior, and now you have to bridge the clicker before continuing the training timeline.

To Assist in Training a Handler – Yes, Really

When I teach a student, and they are just not getting the timing right or cannot read the dog's behavior, I will use the clicker. Then I can mark the dog's correct behavior, and the new handler can concentrate and watch the desired behavior. If the handler is expected to handle the dog, read body language, and mark at the right time, it adds up to a lot they are trying to concentrate on during the session. That's when timing can go out the window. By taking the marking away from the handler, I am reducing the amount he/she needs to concentrate on, which frees up the ability to watch the dog's body language instead. Now, when I click, the handler can observe what the dog is doing and understand better when the correct behavior occurs. Of course, as the clicker is a consistent sound, it doesn't matter to the dog who operates the device, as long as the click happens.

Just Another Gimmick?

I first saw the clicker in the mid-1990s on a VHS videocassette (for the younger readers, a VHS was a large plastic cartridge that, when put into a machine connected to the TV, enabled you to watch the recorded film). Alec Coull, mentioned previously, gave me this VHS tape to watch, having sent it over to England from the States. It was the first time I had ever seen clicker training or anything like it. I still remember viewing the dog being taught agility by using a touch stick and clicker. The trainer led and instructed the dog to touch the end of a stick with its nose. He then moved the stick along a catwalk and gave verbal command to the dog to touch the end of the stick, which it did. As the dog touched the stick, it received a click and a reward. The trainer then continued moving the end of the stick over the catwalk, and the dog followed. At the time, I thought this was all a load of rubbish and another gimmicky dog training trick. How wrong I was!

In the late 1990's I took charge of a Mine Detection Dog project and had several challenges to overcome for the success of the project. One challenge was how to train the dog to search a 50-meter x 1-meter path with the dog's nose covering 100% of the ground, and with the sides of the safe-lane marked with either pin markers or spray paint. We tried several techniques, but the most appropriate way was for the handler to have the dog on a short lead and then direct the dog along the path methodically and under control. Then I had an idea. I remembered the clicker videos loaned to me a couple of years previously, the same ones that I had dismissed as circus tricks. I remembered the part of the video where a guy was using a target stick (touch stick) to guide his dog over a hurdle and catwalk by telling the dog to "touch" and the dog putting its nose on the red ball at the end of the stick. And my epiphany was to wonder what if I taught the dogs to touch their nose at the end of a stick and then move the stick in a left-right-left zigzag pattern along the ground in front of the handler. I thought that the technique would allow the handler to control the dog and ensure its nose covered 100% of the ground. I gathered the three soldiers assigned to the project into a room and explained to them clicker training and the touch stick concept. One soldier in particular, Wes, asked in his broad Northern Irish accent, "have you lost your #@** marbles, Sarge?" (meaning "are you crazy, Sergeant?"). I immediately told Wes to bring me one of his dogs. There were six dogs on the team, all Labradors, and he could have picked any one of them. Luckily for me, he chose a natural at learning clicker training who also loved cheese, as typically Labs do. I quickly did some bridging to the clicker and started to shape the touch stick. The dog was excellent and that same day it was chasing the stick to put its nose on the end; in fact, I couldn't keep up with its behavior and had to take breaks as I was running out of treats. It is fair to say the guys were impressed, and the next morning Wes came into work having rushed into town after the clicker demonstration. He bought three clickers and never looked back.

Using the Clicker

I prefer the simple box clickers that are cheap and easy to replace. I have a box full of them as I get them custom-made with my company logo on them. There are many variations available now, so just get one you like. However, be aware that some dogs dislike the click sound the box clickers make. So, if your dog doesn't like it, just use something else. There are phone apps that are clickers or other devices with volume controls. You can also use something like a jar lid that has the security dimple on it. Once the jar is opened, they click! You could even consider the use of a whistle and replace the clicker completely. It doesn't matter as long as it works for you and your dog.

Remember, when using the clicker (or another device) you must always reward a click. However, the reward doesn't need to be the highest value, especially when using a variable reward system. If you make a mistake and click when you didn't mean to, then don't reward with cheese but instead use a "good dog" verbal reward (or other low value reward) and move on. The reward is there but is a lower value reward instead of a jackpot or other high value reward. A behavior is more likely to be repeated if the reward is of high value, since it accelerates learning, so using a low value reward in this case does not accelerate the learning of the behavior you didn't mean to click.

I attached my clicker to a lanyard so I can wear it around my neck when training. I like my hands free of anything and holding the clicker in my hand would just get in the way. Some versions can be worn with a wrist strap or even attached to your finger, like a ring.

Remember, once bridged the dog understands the concept that the click means reward is imminent. Therefore, your job is to mark (click) at the exact moment the dog performs a behavior you want to capture. The moment the click happens, the learning phase is over, and now the dog must be rewarded. So, as previously mentioned, timing of the click is critical. In this training program, the click serves no other purpose than to mark a behavior. It should not be used as a method of recall when out with your dog, as in clicking over and over to get your dog to return. The clicker should ONLY be used to mark behaviors during a training session, particularly during the next 15 days.

There is no need to point the clicker at the dog when you use it. If you do use a lanyard around the neck, it's not even an option to point the clicker at the dog (depending on the length of the lanyard). Consider this: the clicker does nothing but make a sound, so pointing it at your dog does not project special magical powers at your dog.

When you use the clicker, it should be a quick tik-tok sound, no pause in-between the two sounds. To achieve the quick consecutive sound, be certain to press the metal piece and let it go again!

I use treats as the clicker reward. Typically, the "jackpot" treat determined during the selection assessment is used. You just need small pieces of the treat. You don't want to fill the dog's stomach, so it feels too full to train. So small, 1/3" x 1/3" (1cm x 1cm) sized pieces or smaller work best. Some commercial training treats are already the right size for training.

There, it's that simple!

Grey Behavior

Well, it would be if people (us humans) were not involved at times. One of the most critical factors here is timing and human error can present challenges. If your timing is off, you send the wrong communication, and you will get "grey behavior."

Grey behavior is a term I use when your communication is not black and white, so the dog doesn't quite understand the required behavior. The result is sloppy behavior and not because the dog is lazy, but because your communication has confused the behavior, and the dog is providing the best interpretation it can. For instance, if you want a sit at the heel with the dog in an upright position but you "click" when the dog is slumped a couple of times, sitting crooked a couple of times, sitting slightly behind you a couple of times...then you are going to a get a "grey behavior" because the dog understands any one of those positions as a "sit" and that offering a variation may result in a reward. Poor timing is one reason we have for grey behavior, and the easiest solution is only to mark the behavior you want, and not accept behavior that is close-ish to the goal of the training session.

Plan for Success

Clicker training is a very versatile tool to have available if you need it. It is also great for imprinting, and I enjoy how quickly and easily it communicates to the dog what behavior will be rewarded. This training is designed to be consistent and instantaneous in the communication (as long as your clicking is timed correctly). At the same time, it is forgiving. If you click incorrectly, give a low value reward; just don't do it too many times.

This workbook aims to imprint your dog in 15 days. The level of clicker training described here is basic and only designed to assist in the imprinting process. You can continue to utilize the clicker in other forms of training (I do this a lot). Now that the dog has been bridged, you have the tool pre-loaded. There are plenty of resources available online to continue your clicker journey. I also post videos to my social media accounts which you may use as reference for further training.

If you are ever at one of my presentations, courses, or seminars, I will give you a free clicker just for purchasing this book. I would like to say something like, "that's a $9.99 value!" But we all know it is not!

Stick to the plan! Do not short cut or think, "the dog's got it, think I'll move on." Just complete the progression plan entirely.

Now, let's clicker train the dog. It is a straightforward process and will provide an opportunity for you to practice timing with the clicker while at the same time bridging the sound to your dog.

Training Plan, Lesson 3

Lesson Overview			
Event	Clicker Introduction	Day	2/3
		Lesson No.	3
Equipment	Clicker – or chosen marker system Treats Treat pouch or container Chair (if preferred)		
Location	Indoor room with minimal distractions		
Duration	4 x 10 minutes		
Aim	To bridge the clicker as a marker		
Objectives	To bridge the clicker (or chosen marker) to a reward To use the clicker at the correct time To practice using the clicker without having to think about it		
Prerequisite Lesson	Treat Reward Selection Assessment	Prerequisite Lesson No.	2
Setup	Prepare treats selected for the training event. The dog should be off lead. Have the treats readily available either in a pouch or a container close to hand. Ensure clicker (chosen marker) functions correctly. If using a chair, position it with the back against a wall. Have a bowl of water available in the training area.		
Remarks			
Quick Look			

Training Plan, Lesson 3 (pg. 2)

Steps to Success	
Step	**Action**
1	Sit in a chair facing an area approximately 15 feet x 15 feet or larger.
2	Take a few pieces of treat into your hand and the clicker in the other, ready to use.
3	When the dog is looking at you, throw a treat to the side.
4	When the dog is just about to eat it – its mouth is just about to touch the treat – click!
5	Repeat steps 3 and 4, completing the number of repetitions specified for the subtask in the progression plan below.
6	Take at least a 15-minute break between sessions, going for a walk and allowing your dog to relax.
7	Once your dog has successfully completed 2 sessions (with breaks), move to the next subtask.

Progression Plan			
Task	**Subtask**	**Description**	**Number of treats/clicks**
1		**Bridge the Clicker**	
	1.1	Throw a treat on the floor at least 6 feet left and right of the handler. Click just as the dog eats the treat.	15
	1.2	Throw a treat on the floor at least 6 feet left and right of the handler. Click just as the dog eats the treat.	10
	1.3	Throw treats on the floor vary distances left and right of the handler. Click just as the dog eats treats.	15

Progress Check Lesson 3	
Does the dog maintain interest and eat the treats for the duration of the session?	Yes/No
If no, repeat Subtask 1.2 and reassess.	

Note: If the dog does not maintain interest for the duration, change the treats for something more rewarding to the dog or use various treats (cheese, bacon, chicken) during each session.

Training Plan, Lesson 4

Lesson Overview			
Event	Clicker Confirmation	Day	4
		Lesson No.	4
Equipment	Clicker – or chosen marker system Treats Treat pouch or container Chair (if preferred)		
Location	Indoor room with minimal distractions		
Duration	3 x 10 minutes		
Aim	To bridge the clicker as a marker		
Objectives	To confirm the bridging of the clicker (or chosen marker) to a reward To use the clicker at the correct time To practice using the clicker without having to think about it		
Prerequisite Lesson	Clicker Introduction	Prerequisite Lesson No.	3
Setup	Prepare treats selected for the training event. The dog should be off lead. Have the treats readily available either in a pouch or a container close to hand. Ensure clicker (chosen marker) functions correctly. If using a chair, position it with the back against a wall. Have a bowl of water available in the training area.		
Remarks			

Training Plan, Lesson 4 (pg. 2)

	Steps to Success
Step	**Action**
1	Sit in a chair facing an area approximately 15 feet x 15 feet or larger.
2	Take a few pieces of treat into your hand and the clicker in the other, ready to use.
3	Allow the dog to walk around the room.
4	Click when the dog is not paying attention and when it looks to you, throw the treat.
5	Repeat steps 3 and 4, completing the number of repetitions specified for the subtask in the progression plan below.
6	Take at least a 15-minute break, going for a walk and allowing your dog to relax.
7	Once your dog has successfully completed two sessions (with breaks), move to the next subtask.

		Progression Plan	
Task	**Subtask**	**Description**	**Number of treats/clicks**
2		**Confirm the Clicker**	
	2.1	Allow the dog to walk around the room. Click when it is not paying attention. Throw a treat 6 feet away when it looks in your direction.	9
	2.2	Allow the dog to walk around the room. Click when it is not paying attention. Throw a treat 6 feet away when it looks in your direction.	7
	2.3	Allow the dog to walk around the room. Click when it is not paying attention. Throw the treat varying distances away when it looks in your direction.	5

Progress Check Lesson 4	
Does the dog turn to face you when you click?	Yes/No
If no, repeat Subtask 2.3 and reassess.	

NOTES

CHAPTER 4 – ODOR SELECTION

I am going to assume that you are reading this book because you want to imprint your dog. Perhaps you already know the odor target you will be using, or maybe that's a decision yet to be made. Either way, it is essential to understand some odor selection principles and how to avoid pitfalls that can influence the overall quality of training and standards. Odor selection is another example of the influence of the 1% Rule, except it is actually larger than 1%. In fact, without the correct selection of the target, you may as well train on a soda can. I keep repeating that dog training is about communication. In this case, communication is critical because without the dog understanding what odor it should be responding to, you will never be successful outside of training. Even if the dog smells the source, without the understanding that it leads to a reward, they will move on. In this chapter, I will provide some basic principles about odor selection and sourcing.

The first question you need to ask yourself is, what is the odor you want to train your dog to find? It seems a simple question, but I have experienced programs where the humans' expectations were way out of line compared to the cognitive ability of a dog. I have seen people place marzipan blocks out as training odor because it smells something like Frangex (a type of gelignite explosive). Or a sack of clothes washing powder and then got upset the dog didn't respond to it correctly and alert on it. When I asked what the handler thought would happen, he stated, "it's supposed to simulate a homemade explosive, so I thought he would find it." Seems unbelievable, but these are real incidents, and I have plenty more examples.

There may be a requirement for permits, licenses, and approvals for specific odor samples. It is impossible to cover the particular requirements for your odor, especially when related to different regions. You need to ensure you understand the requirements and are authorized to procure your samples.

I have not used pseudo or simulated scent products other than in research trials where the substance was being tested. If you do use these products, then the principles below are just as relevant. The manufacturer may have specific requirements for their products, such as the temperature range in which they must be stored.

The Communication Chain of Detection

Before we get into sourcing your target odor, I want to discuss the communication chain of detection. I teach the concept in my presentations as I feel it is essential to understand. If there is an issue in your dog detecting a target, you can investigate each link in the chain to find the missing one and, therefore, the break.

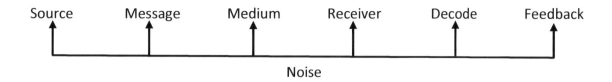

Source	This is the origin of the message; in the case of detection, the message's source will be the item you are looking for. If this part is missing, then the whole process doesn't happen, and there is no way your dog will respond to odor because it doesn't exist. No odor, no detection!
Message	This is the communication leaving the source, and in the case of detection, this is the odor. Clearly, the odor must leave the source for it to be detected. It can be within the headspace immediately at the source or dissipate away from the source.
Medium	This is the way the message (odor) is transported through the environment. It could be a scent cone/plume or even through the soil. If the movement method is blocked somehow, the message will be stopped from transporting the message.
Receiver	In this case, we are talking about the dog's nose and olfactory system. The dog could be sick, old age or just not searching when the odor enters the olfactory system. It could be that there is too little amount for the dog to receive sufficient to analyze.
Decoding	The understanding of the message and we need the dog to analyze the odor and interpret it as target or not target. If the dog knows the odor, it can decode it and understand it is a rewardable opportunity. At this stage in training, we build the relationship between the odor and the reward.
Feedback	The dog's response to the odor (alert, indication). It is the way the dog communicates to us that it has recognized the odor. In most cases, this will be a distinct trained response, and indeed, in the imprinting phase, that is what we want to see—whether that response is taught or the development of natural behavior.
Noise	All of the environmental effects at play during this process and potentially contaminating or disrupting the message. The term noise can cover many things, including scent, sounds, and sights as distractions. Noise can interfere with the communication chain but won't necessarily break a link. We introduce these types of distractions in the training system to reduce their impact in real life.

This communication chain of detection is a visualization of what is happening during the search process and imprinting. If training is struggling, examine each link and determine where the chain is broken.

Odor Procurement

Where you procure your odor is the next question after what your target odor will be. There are several avenues to consider when looking at sources:

- Direct from the origin
- From a third party
- From field finds

Direct from the Origin

For manufactured odor targets, this will be the factory or location the material is manufactured.

- Provides you the purest and freshest form of the odor.
- Has a low contamination risk (unless contamination happens at the source, which then means it belongs as part of the scent picture)
- Arrives in original packaging.
- Lasts longer for both use and storage.
- May not represent field/street versions of the odor. Think about pure cocaine: it is nothing like street cocaine cut many times with contaminants.

From a Third Party

- Can be as pure and fresh as from the source (but not always.)
- Could contain some contamination (but not always).
- Could be in the original packaging (but not always).
- May have a long shelf life after purchase (but not always).
- Will not represent field/street versions.
- May be a little more expensive but easier to source if the origin is outside your country.

From Field Finds

- An accurate representation of the target.
- May have contamination as part of its scent picture.
- May have reduced shelf life.

If available, the odor samples should be tested by a laboratory to confirm quality and verify the samples are free from contamination. However, laboratory testing may not be available to everyone, but something to consider doing if possible.

Facilitating Generalization

I prefer to get a variety of odor sources both from the original source and from the field. As a minimum, I want three variations of each type and at different ages. The generalization to odor will occur if you expose the dog to various odor targets from multiple sources. If you only use one odor type from the same source, you will produce a dog that finds THAT particular odor and may ignore other variants despite them being the same to us. Using as many variations as possible of the same odor type, you imprint the dog on the full range of potential exposures it will encounter. When I start imprinting, I will use the purest form of the odor to ensure the dog receives the most precise communication of what it should be looking for. Once I am confident it understands the association, I will start to vary the samples so that generalization can occur.

Logistical Considerations

Rotation of the odor is important to consider, as rotation frequency may influence what target odor you choose and how you source it. Each odor will have different rotation requirements related to storage and training use and shelf life. If you are storing a target odor in a freezer and using it once a month, it may last a lot longer than something stored under your desk and used daily. The next chapter will discuss storage and handling. You will need a supplier or a source you trust, and that can provide the amount of odor substances you want on the timeline you need. Sometimes this is accomplished through formal arrangements, such as purchase orders, or an arrangement such as an agreement allowing a percentage of finds from each field survey to be kept for canine training. If you need odor for something simple like snakes (for example), I've had success on social media. Also, since snakes are prevalent in Texas, I get plenty of samples to choose from locally. Another practice in gaining odor sources for some organic/live targets is breeding them; for example, if you are in the bed bug detection field, you can breed your own. I do know of handlers who (legally) keep live reptile specimens (legally) at home. Just remember, the reptile will have an odor based on the environment it lives in (a tank) and the food it eats (shop purchased crickets, for example). Generalization is still essential.

Quantity requirements and availability of the odor to procure will be a consideration. In certain situations, oil detection being one of them, the requirement tends to be 10ml of the target for training. Generally, I have to purchase much more than that as such tiny amounts are not sold. In this case, I try to coordinate with one of the clients and get some direct from the refinery as they pull small samples often for quality control. However, at the moment, I have 2 gallons of Texas Intermediate Crude oil and I will never use all of it, but that's the smallest amount I could locate for purchase when I needed some.

Consider the delivery timeline of the odor if you are ordering from a source. Recently I was on a project that required a specialized odor. Initial inquiries before the project started indicated a speedy turnaround and overnight delivery. After the project began, the odor was ordered, and the original delivery window turned into weeks, delaying the project. If you are relying on field finds, this could take even longer.

Using a Neutral Odor for Training

One question I do get asked is what odor I start with. Well, typically, I use KONG, and there several reasons for this:

- It is cheap
- Its odor is consistent
- It is easy to obtain
- It stores well, easy to handle and transport
- It is resilient to all weathers
- It can easily be cut to reduce the size (therefore odor)

You can complete all the training without using the actual target odor. Sounds strange, but when you search for a critically endangered species and training samples are scarce, it is essential. You do not want to use the valuable resource on the initial steps in the training plan. It is better to fully train the dog on a neutral odor, and then, after a quick transfer to target odor, you are ready at a trained standard and have not wasted a lot of valuable target odor. It can also be advantageous if you do not know the final target scent and need to train the dog anyway.

If you have a training issue and need to complete some refresher training, using the KONG is fast and flexible, as you can simply grab it from your training bag and place it out. There is no need for special storage or permits or driving back to your facility to get the target odor from the storage building.

To clean KONG and ensure it is not contaminated with packing, transportation, store, or even your own odors is a simple task. Once it has been cut to the required size, boil the pieces for five minutes in sterile water. Then sieve with a stainless-steel food sieve (cleaned) and air dry in a location without strong odors. Store the dried KONG pieces in a cleaned glass jar. I use stainless-steel tongs/tweezers when handling the KONG pieces so that there is no human odor contamination. Once used, place the pieces in a labeled glass jar ready for recleaning once you have enough to make it worth it. KONG pieces must be cleaned after every use.

Not everyone wants to train on KONG, and that's understandable. If you are not comfortable doing it, then don't. A neutral odor of any type generally has the same advantages. Bear in mind that some neutral odor sources purchased for training can be expensive and have low shelf life.

Availability of Odor and Odor Selection

All of this begs the question, what odor do you start on? Some schools of thought start the dog on the odor with the lowest vapor pressure (and therefore the least amount of odor available to the dog) so that all other odors are easier to detect. Others say start on the highest to get the concept of detection in the dog first. Sometimes you are constrained by the training and have to train with what you have, what you have been given, or what you can get. The question is best answered based on the targets you are teaching. A word of warning, some targets have extremely low vapor pressure and therefore are not suitable for the imprinting phase (pure cocaine, for instance). The profile is just too inconsistent to make imprinting reliable. You must use an odor that provides a consistent odor at a level the dog can detect.

It is essential to understand that surface area has a direct relationship to the odor available. So, if you have one pound of a substance and spread it over a one-foot square, you will have a lot more surface area than, say, if the same amount was in a glass jar that's only 6" in diameter. They are both of the same weight (one pound) and the same substance, but the larger surface area allows more odor to escape and become available to the dog. With that in mind, if you have a small amount of odor but can spread it thinly on a surface, you will have much more target odor for the dog to detect.

Quality Odor for Quality Training

Sourcing your odor is essential, and I will go as far as to say it is critical. Without taking this step with diligence and ensuring you are obtaining the best odor possible, you are risking your dog's standards and efficiency and thus wasting your time and effort during training. The odor is the first link in the communication chain of detection, and if that link is missing, the rest of the chain cannot execute. Ensuring you communicate to your dog what the target odor is will pay dividends in the field. Get the best target odor samples you can!

NOTES

CHAPTER 5 — ODOR STORAGE AND HANDLING

"By failing to prepare, you are preparing to fail."
— Benjamin Franklin, Founding Father of the United States

If we know that the target odor's quality is critical, it follows that handling and storage of the target odor is of great importance. There is no point procuring excellent samples and then throwing them in a cardboard box in the cupboard of a house. Poor storage and handling will introduce contaminants to the target odor; therefore, the training and more importantly the trained standards will be negatively affected.

In storage protocols, we ensure the target and interferent odors are protected from the environment, and the environment is protected from the odors.

I said I would not fill this workbook with science, but I will reference a paper that I believe is essential. I am named a co-author, and it is based on a hypothesis I had from my experiences training at a large military dog school. There were two issues that I felt were ripe for investigation. Firstly, the dogs were always trained on targets of precisely the same weight. This was because the military at this particular school did not allow the cutting of targets into smaller-sized samples. Additionally, the same few buildings were used every day for training. I believed that if you train a dog on a set amount of target and nothing else, that is what the dog would find. Because the target odors would sit in place for 6 hours during a training day, the odors would permeate the wood and become ingrained in the environment. This builds a baseline of odor that the dog learns to ignore because it is continuously present and not rewardable. Based on those experiences and thoughts, I also believed that you could train a dog to a particular threshold level of odor and teach it to ignore larger and smaller amounts of the target. When an opportunity arose to have the concepts studied, Dr. Nathan Hall of Texas Tech University accepted the research project to investigate my theories and assumptions.

The resulting research was published as: Stimulus Control of Odorant Concentration: Pilot Study of Generalization and Discrimination of Odor Concentration in Canines (DeChant, Bunker, Hall, 2021). The paper will be posted to the workbook website page so you can read it in detail if you wish. In brief terms, it was proven that dogs could learn to ignore target odor concentrations outside of the threshold ranges for which they were trained. It also demonstrated that if a baseline of target odor exists in the training areas, dogs will ignore this level of target odor and therefore ignore it in the field. This illustrates how handling target samples and preventing contamination is essential; otherwise, you reduce your detection dogs' standards for no other reason than not following a few basic protocols.

I have rigorous storage and handling protocols which may well be more than you need in your program. Odor detection is the main focus of my business, and I do a lot of research and evaluation projects, so I need to be very meticulous in every way. The principles are precisely the same for me and anyone else that does detection training; therefore, what you will learn in this chapter is best practices which you can adapt to suit your particular needs.

The type of target(s) you work with will, in large part, direct you as to how you store them. Of course, if any regulations, policies, and legal requirements apply, these will give you direct guidance as to how you are to store your target. Some targets need to be frozen to maintain their shelf life, and therefore you have no choice but to use a freezer. I mainly keep training targets in the freezer, although some targets cannot be frozen and therefore the use of a freezer is out. Some may be hazardous, so they must be contained in special lockers and/or containers. Some things such as lizards and fungi must be kept in special tanks to keep them alive. When choosing storage methods, you should consider any requirements as well as convenience—no point buying a freezer if your target is water for pipeline leaks.

For a visual presentation of the techniques described below, you may want to watch my "Handling and Storage of Canine Training Aids" webinar, found on my website.

Storage

There are a few considerations when it comes to how you store your samples and also how you use them in imprinting and training. You have to be aware that the containers you use to store the samples have their own odor. Container odor can become part of the scent picture through absorption by the sample, so it is important to use containers that do not have a strong odor of their own. It also should not be a more pungent odor than the sample. Even if you use the same container for your distractors, you run the risk that finding the container odor will become the dog's primary detection method.

During the Mine Detection Dog project, we imprinted the dogs on 0.025gm (0.00088oz) of TNT, which was melted onto a filter paper. The TNT was the size of a pinhead. During the imprinting, the dogs would work with a training platform and tube system. Eight platforms (approximately 18" high x 36" wide) were made, capable of holding seven metal tubes each. The tubes would contain distractors, TNT on filter papers, and distractors mixed with TNT on the papers. The dogs were required to achieve 100% detection before they could progress to exterior searches. When we transitioned outside, I placed TNT on small open holes in the ground. The dogs were worked on a short lead and a target stick, as described in Chapter 3, in the same style as the rack system. However, the first time we did this, the dogs walked over the TNT without a single response. But what I noticed was that at the holes in which I placed filter papers as distractors; the dogs would pause, investigate and move on. I emplaced a filter paper with TNT on it and worked the dogs again; 100% detection! It was the paper filter the dogs were looking for, then discriminating which had TNT and which didn't. This would not be effective in the field and was resolved by using just TNT and no more TNT on filter papers. A valuable lesson about containers: do not use something that becomes the primary source of detection.

We must also protect the samples from the dog and the dog from the samples in many cases. This is particularly true during imprinting if you are not using a neutral odor. As the dog learns the new behaviors of responding on a target, it is more likely to interact with the sample, even if it's just a nose touch or lick.

Some samples will come with safety data sheets and storage instructions, and they should be followed as they are there for safety and to aid shelf life.

Temperature

Temperature can have an adverse effect on the odors. Heating the samples will make the molecules more volatile and produce more vapor. While this might be good for training, it can mean that your sample is drying out and becoming weaker during storage. When possible, I like to keep my odors in a freezer in order to prevent issues caused by higher temperatures.

Sunlight

Direct sunlight will have effects similar to higher temperatures, but the sun can also destroy bacteria and organisms which can alter the scent picture of your samples. Keeping samples out of the direct sun will prevent damage and also extend their shelf life.

Humidity

Some samples may absorb humidity and therefore alter their consistency and, again, the original scent picture. Humidity can also aid the growth of mold and bacteria.

Pests

Ants, rats, mice, and similar pests would destroy any edible samples and contaminate them with urine and feces.

Other odors

I was once on a training course where training aids were located next to the cleaner's cupboard. When the dogs on the course were taken to a school for training in a real-life environment, they responded on the cleaning cupboard. The industrial floor wax was the same as that used by the dog training school and had become part of the scent picture of the targets. Ensure your odors are not stored near other strong odors.

Security

Security is an obvious consideration for explosives and drugs, but we should protect all our samples. Curious people could decide to look at your samples and cause contamination by handling them without following correct protocols. Additionally, rare, attractive, or interesting samples could be taken as souvenirs.

Store interferents/targets separately

No matter how you ultimately decide to store your samples, keep targets and interferents separate. Cross-contamination between the target and interferents will cause adverse results in your training.

Primary Containers

The primary containers are those that hold the target sample. There are many options for primary storage, and as with the rest of the methods you use, it will depend on your sample. Some examples are described in the chart below.

Type	Pro	Con
Zip top plastic bags	<ul><li>Cheap and easy to replace.</li><li>Allows the odor to breathe so it can be used without taking the sample out of the Ziplock.</li><li>Protects the sample from dirt, moisture, and contamination.</li></ul>	<ul><li>They can add an odor that will become the primary scent for detection more potent than your source.</li></ul>
Glass jars *Borosilicate glass is medical grade and very low odor, so great for things like biomedical samples.	<ul><li>Cheap and easy to replace.</li><li>Very low odor (depending on the lid construction).</li><li>Easy to clean and tolerates aggressive decontamination (Alcohol, Acetone).</li><li>Protects from dirt and contamination (while the lid is on).</li></ul>	<ul><li>Fragile.</li><li>Not so easy to store larger jars.</li></ul>

	• Can add a metal screen to prevent dogs getting to sample.	
Plastic jars/containers	• Cheap and easy to replace. • Low odor (depending on the material used). • Easy to clean. • Protects from dirt and contamination (while lid is on).	• Can crack and break in use, especially as it ages or is exposed to weather variations. • Can have a pungent odor. • Can absorb scent into the material. • Can be damaged or absorb aggressive cleaning agents.
Mylar bags	• Relatively cheap and easy to replace. • Protects the sample from dirt, moisture, and contamination.	

There are plenty of options for storage containers. These are just some examples, and you can apply the same simple criteria to assess your containers and ensure they are fit for your purpose.

Intermediate Containers

The intermediate container is the item you use to hold the primary container which holds the sample. Intermediate containers are going to be very much dependent on your target and the primary container. I use glass jars as my primary containers in most cases and then plastic ammunition cans to hold the jars. You could place your sample in a Ziplock and the Ziplock inside a glass jar.

The containers aim to protect your sample from the environment and the environment from your sample. The multi-layer approach is better than using just one container. In the webinar mentioned above, I tested several containers with a target odor secured inside, and my dog detected each sample correctly despite the containers remaining closed.

Container preparation

I use the same types of containers for the target odors as I do the interferents and prepare them for use and clean them all the same way. Everything is the same except for what's inside the containers. For example, the glass jars are washed, and heat dried in a dishwasher twice, once with soap and once without. This way, I know all the contaminants from production, transportation, and storage are gone. The jars all have the same preparation smell (if any), and they are all at the same odor baseline level. If the container cannot tolerate machine washing, I will hand wash, rinse and air dry.

I once stored some target odors in glass jars in a fridge, but I would store the interferents on a shelf in a different room because the fridge had limited space. In training as the dogs would achieve 100% detection of the target, and things were going great. Then I decided to use some seaweed as the interferent (I do a lot of beach searches), and because it is organic and rots, I put it in the fridge. In the next training session, I placed out the target odor, the interferents from the storage shelf, and the seaweed from the refrigerator. The dogs responded on the seaweed. Not just once and they were totally committed responses. So, I placed an empty jar in the fridge, and the next time I worked on them, I put out the interferents and the empty jar from the refrigerator. The dogs responded on the fridge jar and again, with committed responses. I had made the fridge smell part of the odor picture!

Barriers

Barriers are used to protect the sample from the environment and the environment from the sample. Barriers can be made from various materials and I generally use natural items if the sample is disposable, like crude oil. That way, after training I just burn both the sample and the barrier I used. However, if the sample is used more than once, then I want to make sure the barrier doesn't have an odor that would affect the target scent. Typical barriers are aluminum foil, greaseproof paper, cardboard, and paper. They may be more robust such as plastic trays, Tupperware containers, and metal boxes.

The barrier needs to be low/no odor to prevent it from contaminating the samples.

Once an item has been used as a barrier, it should be destroyed or only ever used for that same target in the future.

Gloves

Using gloves to handle samples is something I cannot stress enough. I have heard people make statements such as "a terrorist doesn't wear gloves!" However, a terrorist isn't training detection dogs, and there are many reasons you should not only use gloves but use them effectively.

We want to protect the samples (target and interferent/blank) from human odor and to protect ourselves from the target. Explosives, for instance, are chemicals that can cause medical issues if absorbed into the body (Gad, 2014). Back in my early days of training, we never used gloves and I would get raging headaches if I handled C-4 (USA)/PE-4 (UK), an RDX based explosive. We also knew that nitroglycerine explosives would contaminate anything it touched. On days we were training nitro, we only ever signed that out of the storage bunker and no other explosives.

We also do not want to add contamination odor to the target and make that part of the scent picture. If a limited number of people are handling the samples, then their scents will repeatedly be impregnated into the items. Strong odors on hands (smoking, oil, perfume, food, sanitizer) can transfer to the target and be absorbed to become part of the scent picture. Remember the experience I had with TNT on filter papers; do not needlessly add human scent into the scent picture.

Types of gloves

Gloves are made from several materials, and the most common for dog training use are described below.

Type	Description	Advantages	Protection level
Latex	Natural rubber	Comfortable, flexible, and sensitive feel	Bacteria and virus
Nitrile	Synthetic	Stretches and durable	Chemical and virus
Vinyl	Synthetic	Cheaper option and comfortable	Chemical
Polyethylene	Synthetic	Cheap, low odor, easy to take off	Low

Gloves have a limited shelf life and storing them in direct sunlight or higher temperatures will reduce the life.

Powder-free versions are advantageous as they do not leave powder (contamination) on the items you are handling.

Chlorinated gloves have an odor and should not be used.

Principles of use of gloves

- Use fresh, clean gloves each time you handle samples.
- Select glove type based on fit and use.

- Check gloves before use (tears, cracks).
- Use separate gloves to handle targets or interferent and do not mix them.
- Take off to open doors, containers, places of concealment, etc.
- Dispose of gloves soon as possible.
- Do not use the same gloves for different training aids.
- Dispose of gloves if compromised.

By using disposable gloves, you will preserve your samples' life and effectiveness and improve the quality of your training standards—just another one of the 1% Rule advantages.

Handling

Tongs and tweezers can be used for handling the samples. I use medical grade stainless steel items, and they are cleaned with acetone and air dried after each use.

Cross-contamination

Cross-contamination is the tainting of the sample by other odors or particles (soil, water, dust, etc.) and the sample tainting the environment.

- Always start with clean containers.
- Always wear a fresh pair of disposable gloves when handling the training samples and training aids. Discard the gloves after use and before handling other training samples/aids (or anything else, for that matter).
- Never allow your dog to come into direct contact with the training samples.
- Do not handle the training samples/aid unnecessarily.
- Keep training samples/aids separate from one another.
- Once a container has been used for a particular odor, confine its use solely to that odor.

Handling Odor Containers During Training

I follow a strict sequence every time I open a container and remove a sample of target odor:

1. Place the barrier at the hide location and make sure doors, drawers, *etc.* are open so you can enter and plant the target without touching anything.
2. Collect and carry the intermediate container with clean ungloved hands.
3. Place the container in a location outside the search area.
4. Open the container.
5. Put on disposable gloves.
6. Take out the primary container.

7. Open the primary container at the location of the hide.
8. Place the target on a barrier.
9. Close the primary container and return it to the intermediate container.
10. Remove the gloves and close the container.
11. When the odor is secured, clean the outside of the intermediate container and hands with disinfecting wipes.

To collect the target once training is completed, you repeat the process.

When you open an intermediate container within a training area, you are potentially causing a plume of odor to come out of the container and remain in the location. Sometimes this may be an advantage but generally, it is not. For instance, if I am training a dog with little training or experience on an inside search, I may open the container within the room containing the target hide. As the dog enters the room, it will start to detect particles of target odors in the air, and this "hint" will drive it to search harder and find the source. However, I may not want to provide this hint in other training exercises, so I open the intermediate container away from the training location. Then I carry the primary container into the hide location, open it there, and plant the sample.

Post-Training Routine

Cleaning the area after training should be part of your routine. Remove all odors and barriers and ensure you can account for everything you used that day. Then clean the hide location by use of cleansing agents. Depending on the surface, I use different products: bleach and water on floors, alcohol or acetone on surfaces such as Formica or tile, and Clorox wipes on wooden drawers.

Quality Handling Practices for Quality Training

Storage and handling of the odors are critical to the success of your training and effectiveness in the field. It will save you money in purchasing training samples and interferents to replace those that are damaged or contaminated. It will ensure your training areas are not contaminated, and again, this will aid the team's standards being achieved. It is fair to say that preparation for training takes more time than the training itself. But it will pay dividends in the short and long term.

CHAPTER 6 – TEACHING THE RESPONSE

"Tell me, and I'll forget. Show me, and I may not remember. Involve me, and I'll understand."
Confucius

The final part of the communication chain of detection is "feedback," which is the response the dog provides to locating the target odor. Without a response, the dog cannot communicate that it has found target odor, so we need to ensure we equip it with a reliable and obtainable type of response. There are two ways to develop the response. One is to train a particular behavior. The other is to allow the dog to demonstrate a natural behavior and reinforce it. I prefer to teach a response and generally opt for the sit response. However, if a client or project needs something different, then I will train the desired behavior. For instance, I had a research project that required the dogs to place their nose into a pipe and hold it there for four seconds when they located the target odor. In this case, they were rewarded for the freeze inside the pipe and were allowed to sit or stand as they wanted.

The type of response is a personal decision, although in some cases you will be required to train a specific behavior such as a certification standard, such as a bark response in the case of the Federal Emergency Management Agency (FEMA) canines which are required to give a bark response.

Using KONG to Develop the Response

I use a couple of ways to develop a response, and each has its pros and cons. In this workbook, I will be describing the system to train the response separate from the odor and then transfer it to the target. This method is simple and easy to apply. When applied correctly, the steps are much more progressive and produce the desired goal very quickly and effectively. However, this method uses a neutral odor to develop the response and I use KONG for this purpose. Some people, I was one of them for many years, do not like to use KONG as a training odor, and I can understand the concerns. If you are on a live search and there is a KONG in the area, the dog may respond to it. That risk does exist, of course, however in most applications outside of explosive and drug searches, this isn't a huge deal. If my conservation or environmental dogs find a KONG during a survey, they just saved me $13 on a new toy. But that is quite different than if a response by a dog results in the deployment of a bomb disposal team. Having said that, my dogs, in hundreds of miles of surveys, have never located a KONG.

Advantages	Disadvantages
• Consistent odor • Easily available • It can be cut into tiny pieces • Waterproof • Rot proof	• The dog may alert on a KONG during a real search

• Safe to bury • Can be left in public places • Carried without restriction	

KONG has many advantages, but the one significant disadvantage may mean you do not wish to use it. However, you could replace the KONG with any neutral item you decide to use as long as it is fit for the system.

I use red KONG pieces as this is easy for a human to see in the environment but not so for a dog (due to color perception). KONG's different colors have different odor levels, black being the most odorous and softer KONGs being the least. The compound added to the rubber to make it stronger smells, and the higher amounts means stronger odor. The red color KONG has plenty of odor, but if cutting a red KONG is too hard, you could use pink or purple. They have less of the hardener compound, so have lower odor but are easier to cut.

Cutting KONG can be difficult and takes time; one tip I have is to wet the rubber and keep it wet. Use a sharp knife but, of course, watch your hands. I was fortunate to get KONG material ground into pieces by a machine, which saves lots of hard work and no risk to my fingers.

Response Options

In this program, we will be teaching a sit response. If you want a different response, you just replace the sit development steps for your chosen behavior, down or stand and stare, for instance. You can teach the bark response using the system, but I have not included it in the workbook to prevent confusing the progression plans' flow. However, the training plan process is the same whether it's a sit, down, or bark response.

Clear Communication Goes Both Ways

The response is the final piece of the communication chain and where the dog has communicated that the source has been located. Without the response, you will never know the dog has located the odor, and therefore your detection team is not effective. I have found that during extended searches where the dog has located lots of target locations, the response becomes weaker. The dog gets tired after 10 miles in arduous terrain and 100 target odor locations. So, there may be a deterioration in the response from a sit. For example, a dog may just demonstrate a change in behavior with a "freeze" body position and look towards you. Reading the body language and communication as a dog handler becomes the skill set to make you effective in the field.

However, that does not deter us from ensuring we expect the best response standards during imprinting (the baseline behavior) and into training, maintenance training, and beyond.

Training is training, and we should always expect the behaviors to meet the plan's standards and not accept anything less. It will pay dividends in the field, even if you are completing long, arduous searches and locating many target odors.

Clear communication from you at this stage will provide clear communication from the dog as you continue into training beyond the imprinting phase.

Training Plan, Lesson 5

NOTE: In the following lessons, the term *treat* may be replaced with any reward suitable for your dog. The system will work with a toy reward, although you may need more rest periods due to the physical exercise required in toy play.

Lesson Overview			
Event	Response Training 1 – Lure the sit	Day	4
		Lesson No.	5
Equipment	Treats Treat pouch or container		
Location	Indoor room with minimal distractions		
Duration	10 x 5 minutes		
Aim	To teach the dog the concept of lure to sit		
Objectives	To teach the dog the concept of luring To teach the dog the sit		
Prerequisite Lesson	Clicker Confirmation	Prerequisite Lesson No.	4
Setup	Prepare treats selected for the training event. The dog should be off lead. Have the treats readily available either in a pouch or a container close to hand. Have a bowl of water available in the training area.		
Remarks			
Quick Look			

Training Plan, Lesson 5 (pg. 2)

	Steps to Success
Step	**Action**
1	Hold a piece of treat with your thumb and forefinger.
2	Allow the dog to smell the treat in your hand while it stands in front of you.
3	Keeping the treat close to the dog's nose, raise your hand up and back above its head.
4	(3.1) As the dog's rear end starts to drop towards the sit position, give the treat.
4	(3.2) When the dog reaches the full sit position, give the treat.
4	(3.3) When the dog reaches the full sit position, click and reward with the opposite hand.
4	(3.4) Lure the dog without a treat. When the dog reaches the full sit position, click and reward with opposite hand.
4	(3.5) Lure the dog without a treat. Click once the dog is in the sit position and reward with a treat from pouch/container.
5	Repeat steps 3 and 4, completing the number of repetitions specified for the subtask in the progression plan below. Once your dog has successfully completed two sessions (with breaks), move to the next subtask.

Do not use a cue word (sit, for instance) during this 15-day imprinting process. You are not teaching the behavior on cue for the imprinting program.

		Progression Plan	
Task	**Subtask**	**Description**	**Number of treats/clicks**
3		**Lure to Sit**	
	3.1	Lure the dog towards a sitting position – does not have to be in a full sit at this stage.	4
	3.2	Lure the dog to the sit position	4
	3.3	Lure the dog to the sit position – reward from the opposite hand	3
	3.4	Lure the dog without a treat to the sit position – reward from the opposite hand	3
	3.5	Lure the dog without a treat to the sit position – reward from pouch/container	4

Progress Check	
Does the dog sit with a lure without a treat in the hand?	Yes/No
If no, repeat subtask 3.5 and reassess.	

Training Plan, Lesson 6

NOTE: Moving forward you can choose NOT to use a piece of KONG. You can ignore the KONG and just use the bottle lid. That does mean you do not have the advantages of a KONG odor for future training, especially when you move into search. But if you are not comfortable using KONG as an odor it does not prevent you continuing through the steps of the workbook. You can replace the KONG with a metal washer, coin or any other similar neutral target if you wish.

Lesson Overview			
Event	Response Training 2 – Lure the sit with a bottle lid/KONG	Day	5
		Lesson No.	6
Equipment	Treats Treat pouch or container Plastic pill bottle lid (or similar) Piece of KONG approximately 2" x 2"		
Location	Indoor room with minimal distractions		
Duration	8 x 5 minutes		
Aim	To teach the dog the concept of lure to sit with the bottle lid/KONG		
Objectives	To teach the dog the concept of sit when presented the bottle lid To teach the dog to offer the sit behavior at the bottle lid		
Prerequisite Lesson	Response Training 1 – Lure the sit	Prerequisite Lesson No.	5
Setup	Prepare treats selected for the training event. The dog should be off lead. Have the treats readily available either in a pouch or a container close to hand. Ensure the bottle lid/KONG are cleaned before training. Have a bowl of water available in the training area.		
Remarks			
Quick Look			

Training Plan, Lesson 6 (pg. 2)

	Steps to Success
Step	**Action**
1	Hold the pill bottle lid in your hand with a piece of treat hidden underneath it and a piece of KONG on top.
2	(4.1) Lure the dog into the sit ensuring it can see the bottle lid/KONG. Once in sit drop the treat from behind the bottle lid.
2	(4.2) Move the hand with the bottle lid/KONG away from the dog so the dog follows the hand for about 3 feet. Then stop the hand as the dog approaches and smoothly conduct the luring action to the sit. Drop treat from behind the bottle lid when the dog is in sit position looking at the bottle lid.
2	(4.3) Move the hand with the bottle lid/KONG away from the dog so the dog follows the hand for about 3 feet. Hold the hand still and wait for a sit. If needed, move the hand with bottle lid a small distance up and back but fade as soon as possible.
3	Repeat steps 1 and 2, completing the number of repetitions specified for the subtask in the progression plan below. Once your dog has successfully completed two sessions (with breaks), move to the next subtask.

Do not use a cue word (sit, for instance) during this 15-day imprinting process. You are not teaching the behavior on cue for the imprinting program.

		Progression Plan	
Task	**Subtask**	**Description**	**Number of treats/clicks**
4		**Lure to Sit with the Bottle Lid and KONG**	
	4.1	Lure the dog towards a sitting position with the bottle lid/KONG in the hand used to lure the dog.	4
	4.2	Move the lure hand away from the dog 3 feet and then lure the sit response.	6
	4.3	Move the lure hand away from the dog 3 feet and wait for the sit response.	5

Progress Check	
Does the dog sit after having approached the lure hand that holds the bottle lid/KONG?	Yes/No
If no, repeat subtask 4.3 and reassess.	

Training Plan, Lesson 7

Lesson Overview			
Event	Response Training 3 – Sit and stare at bottle lid/KONG various heights	Day	6
		Lesson No.	7
Equipment	Treats Treat pouch or container Plastic pill bottle lid (or similar) Piece of KONG approximately 2" x 2"		
Location	Indoor room with minimal distractions		
Duration	10 x 5 minutes		
Aim	To teach the dog the concept of sitting with the bottle lid/KONG at various heights		
Objectives	To teach the dog the concept of sit when presented the bottle lid/KONG To teach the dog to offer the sit behavior at the bottle lid/KONG To teach the dog to stare at the bottle lid/KONG To introduce various heights		
Prerequisite Lesson	Response Training 2 – Lure the sit with a bottle lid	Prerequisite Lesson No.	6
Setup	Prepare treats selected for the training event. The dog should be off lead. Have the treats readily available either in a pouch or a container close to hand. Ensure the bottle lid/KONG are cleaned before training. Have a bowl of water available in the training area.		
Remarks			
Quick Look			

Training Plan, Lesson 7 (pg. 2)

Steps to Success	
Step	**Action**
1	Hold the pill bottle lid on your hand with a piece of treat hidden underneath and KONG on top.
2	(5.1) Move the hand with the bottle lid/KONG away from the dog so the dog follows the hand for about 3 feet. Then stop the hand at a height midway between the floor and the dog's head (chest height). When the dog approaches and offers a sit, drop the treat from behind the lid. Ensure the dog is looking at the bottle lid.
2	(5.2) Move the hand with the bottle lid/KONG away from the dog so the dog follows the hand for about 3 feet. Place the bottle lid on the floor with the treat underneath. Keep your finger on the piece of KONG on top of the bottle lid to prevent the dog from self-rewarding or being active in response. Lift the bottle lid to present the treat when the dog offers a sit and is staring at the bottle lid/KONG.
2	(5.3) Move the hand with the bottle lid/KONG away from the dog so the dog follows the hand for about 3 feet. Place the bottle lid on the floor WITHOUT the treat underneath. Keep your finger on the bottle lid/KONG. When the dog offers a sit and is staring at the lid/KONG, drop a treat from above its head. Try to hit the bottle lid/KONG or get as close as you can.
2	(5.4) Move the hand with the bottle lid/KONG away from the dog so the dog follows the hand for about 3 feet. Place the bottle lid/KONG on the floor WITHOUT the treat underneath. Start moving the hand away from the bottle lid/KONG once placed on the ground. When the dog offers a sit and is staring at the bottle lid/KONG, drop a treat from above its head. Try to hit the bottle lid/KONG or get as close as you can.
2	(5.5) Move the hand with the bottle lid/KONG away from the dog so the dog follows the hand for about 3 feet. Place the bottle lid/KONG on the floor WITHOUT the treat underneath. Move the hand away immediately. When the dog offers a sit and is staring at the bottle lid/KONG, drop a treat from above its head. Try to hit the bottle lid/KONG or get as close as you can.
3	Repeat step 2, completing the number of repetitions specified for the subtask in the progression plan below. Once your dog has successfully completed two sessions (with breaks), move to the next subtask.

Do not use a cue word (sit, for instance) during this 15-day imprinting process. You are not teaching the behavior on cue for the imprinting program.

Progression Plan			
Task	Subtask	Description	Number of treats/clicks
5		**Sit and Stare at Bottle Lid/KONG at Various Heights**	
	5.1	Move the hand with the bottle lid 3 feet and stop at chest height.	4
	5.2	Move the hand with the bottle lid/KONG 3 feet and place it on the floor, treat under the bottle lid.	5
	5.3	Move the hand with the bottle lid/KONG 3 feet and place it on the floor without a treat under the bottle lid.	6
	5.4	Move the hand with the bottle lid/KONG 3 feet and place it on the floor without a treat under the bottle lid. Start to fade hand away from the bottle lid.	4
	5.5	Move the hand with the bottle lid/KONG 3 feet and place it on the floor without a treat under the bottle lid. Remove your hand immediately.	5

Progress Check	
Does the dog sit and stare, after having approached the bottle lid/KONG?	Yes/No
If no, repeat from 5.3 and reassess.	

Training Plan, Lesson 8

Lesson Overview			
Event	Response Training 4 – Sit and stare at bottle lid/KONG with duration	Day	7
		Lesson No.	8
Equipment	Treats Treat pouch or container Plastic pill bottle lid (or similar) Piece of KONG approximately 2" x 2"		
Location	Indoor room with minimal distractions		
Duration	8 x 5 minutes		
Aim	To teach the dog the concept of to sit and stare at the bottle lid/KONG with duration		
Objectives	To teach the dog the concept of sit and stare at the bottle lid with duration		
Prerequisite Lesson	Response Training 3 – Lure the sit with bottle lid/KONG at various heights	Prerequisite Lesson No.	7
Setup	Prepare treats selected for the training event. The dog should be off lead. Have the treats readily available either in a pouch or a container close to hand. Ensure the bottle lid/KONG are cleaned before training. Have a bowl of water available in the training area.		
Remarks			
Quick Look			

Steps to Success	
Step	**Action**
1	(6.1) Place the bottle lid/KONG on the floor within sight of the dog and move your hand away. When the dog approaches and offers a sit response, wait 3 seconds and then drop the treat from above the dog. Ensure the dog is looking at the bottle lid/KONG.
1	(6.2) Place the bottle lid/KONG on the floor within sight of the dog and move your hand away. When the dog approaches and offers a sit response, wait 5 seconds and then drop the treat from above the dog. Ensure the dog is looking at the bottle lid/KONG.
1	(6.3) Place the bottle lid/KONG on the floor within sight of the dog and move your hand away. When the dog approaches and offers a sit response, wait 7 seconds, and the drop treat from above the dog. Ensure the dog is looking at the bottle lid/KONG.
1	(6.4) Place the bottle lid/KONG on the floor within sight of the dog and move your hand away. When the dog approaches and offers a sit response, vary the sit-stare duration between 1-7 seconds and then drop the treat from above the dog. Ensure the dog is looking at the bottle lid/KONG.
2	Repeat step 1, completing the number of repetitions specified for the subtask in the progression plan below. Once your dog has successfully completed two sessions (with breaks), move to the next subtask.

Do not use a cue word (sit, for instance) during this 15-day imprinting process. You are not teaching the behavior on cue for the imprinting program.

Progression Plan			
Task	**Subtask**	**Description**	**Number of treats/clicks**
6		**Sit and stare at the Bottle Lid/KONG with duration**	
	6.1	Dog holds a sit and stare at bottle lid/KONG for 3 seconds.	4
	6.2	Dog holds a sit and stare at bottle lid/KONG for 5 seconds.	3
	6.3	Dog holds a sit and stare at bottle lid/KONG for 7 seconds.	5
	6.4	Dog holds a sit and stare at bottle lid/KONG for variable durations between 1-7 seconds.	4

Progress Check	
Does the dog sit and stare, having approached the bottle lid/KONG, for 7 seconds?	Yes/No
If no, repeat from 6.2 and reassess.	

Training Plan, Lesson 9

Lesson Overview			
Event	Response Training 5 – Sit and stare at bottle lid/KONG with duration and marker	Day	8
		Lesson No.	9
Equipment	Clicker (or chosen marker) Treats Treat pouch or container Plastic pill bottle lid (or similar) Piece of KONG approximately 2" x 2"		
Location	Indoor room with minimal distractions		
Duration	6 x 5 minutes		
Aim	To teach the dog to hold response until marked		
Objectives	To reinforce the concept of sit and stare at the bottle lid/KONG with duration To proof the behavior by having you move away from the bottle lid/KONG To teach the dog that the marker ends the response behavior To teach the dog to move away from the source for the reward		
Prerequisite Lesson	Response Training 4 – Sit and stare at bottle lid/KONG with duration	Prerequisite Lesson No.	8
Setup	Prepare treats selected for the training event. The dog should be off lead. Have the treats readily available either in a pouch or a container close to hand. Ensure clicker (marker) functions correctly. Ensure the bottle lid/KONG are cleaned before training. Have a bowl of water available in the training area.		
Remarks			
Quick Look			

Training Plan, Lesson 9 (pg. 2)

	Steps to Success	
Step	**Action**	
1	Place the bottle lid/KONG on the floor within sight of the dog and remove your hand.	
2	(7.1) When the dog approaches and offers a sit, wait 5 seconds and click (mark). Ensure the dog is staring at the bottle lid/KONG when you click.	
2	(7.2) When the dog approaches and offers a sit response, vary the sit stare duration between 1-7 seconds and click. Ensure the dog is staring at the bottle lid/KONG when you click.	
2	(7.3) Stand up and move away from the lid/KONG. When the dog approaches and offers a sit response, vary the sit stare duration between 1-7 seconds and click. Ensure the dog is staring at the bottle lid/KONG when you click.	
3	Repeat steps 1 and 2, completing the number of repetitions specified for the subtask in the progression plan below. Once your dog has successfully completed two sessions (with breaks), move to the next subtask.	

Do not use a cue word (sit, for instance) during this 15-day imprinting process. You are not teaching the behavior on cue for the imprinting program.

	Progression Plan		
Task	**Subtask**	**Task**	**Number of treats/clicks**
7		**Sit and Stare at the Bottle Lid/KONG with duration and end with a click**	
	7.1	Dog approaches the bottle lid/KONG and holds a sit and stare for 3 seconds.	4
	7.2	Dog approaches the bottle lid/KONG and holds a sit and stare for variable durations between 1-7 seconds.	5
	7.3	Dog approaches the bottle lid/KONG and holds a sit and stare for variable durations between 1-7 seconds.	4

Progress Check	
Does the dog sit and stare, having approached the bottle lid/KONG, for 7 seconds, and end behavior on the click?	Yes/No
If no, repeat from 7.2 and reassess.	

Now that you have a passive sit response on the bottle lid/KONG you can remove the lid and use only KONG.

Training Plan, Lesson 10

Lesson Overview			
Event	Response Training 6 – Sit and stare at KONG	Day	9
		Lesson No.	10
Equipment	Clicker (or chosen marker) Treats Treat pouch or container Piece of KONG approximately 2" x 2"		
Location	Indoor room with minimal distractions		
Duration	4 x 5 minutes		
Aim	To teach the dog the concept of to sit and stare at a piece of KONG		
Objectives	To teach the dog the concept of sit and stare at a piece of KONG with duration To teach the dog that the marker ends the response behavior To teach the dog to move away from the source for the reward		
Prerequisite Lesson	Response Training 5 – Sit and stare at bottle lid/KONG with duration and marker	Prerequisite Lesson No.	9
Setup	Prepare treats selected for the training event. The dog should be off lead. Have the treats readily available either in a pouch or a container close to hand. Ensure clicker (marker) functions correctly. Ensure the bottle lid is cleaned before training. Ensure KONG is clean. Have a bowl of water available in the training area.		
Remarks			
Quick Look			

	Steps to Success
Step	**Action**
1	(8.1) Place the KONG on the floor within sight of the dog. Keep a finger on the piece of KONG. If the dog smells the KONG before sitting, that is acceptable. When the dog approaches and offers a sit, wait 3 seconds and click (mark). Ensure the dog is staring at the KONG when you click.
1	(8.2) Place the KONG on the floor within sight of the dog. Move the hand away from the KONG. If the dog smells the KONG before sitting, that is acceptable. When the dog approaches and offers a sit, wait 5 seconds and click (mark). Ensure the dog is staring at the KONG when you click.
1	(8.3) Place the KONG on the floor within sight of the dog, stand up and move away. When the dog approaches and offers a sit response, vary the sit stare duration between 1-7 seconds and click. Ensure the dog is staring at the KONG when you click.
2	Repeat step 1, completing the number of repetitions specified for the subtask in the progression plan below. Once your dog has successfully completed two sessions (with breaks), move to the next subtask.

Do not use a cue word (sit, for instance) to tell the dog what to do. You are not teaching the behavior on cue for the imprinting program.

		Progression Plan	
Task	**Subtask**	**Description**	**Number of treats/clicks**
8		**Sit and stare at KONG with duration, move away and end with a click**	
	8.1	Dog approaches KONG and holds a sit and stare for 3 seconds	4
	8.2	Dog approaches KONG and holds a sit and stare for 5 seconds	3
	8.3	Dog approaches KONG and holds a sit and stare for variable durations between 1-7 seconds	5

Progress Check	
Does the dog sit and stare, having approached the KONG, for 7 seconds and end behavior on the click while you have moved away?	Yes/No
If no, repeat from 8.1 and reassess.	

NOTES

CHAPTER 7 – METHOD OF IMPRINTING

Once the dog has completed the response training and passes the Progress Check for Lesson 10, you can begin imprinting. Imprinting is when we introduce a target odor to a dog and bridge the scent to a behavior (response). In the first stage, I only use one target odor source as I want consistency in learning. Not until the dog has completed this phase and passed the Progress Check will I add different variations of the target odor. I need the dog to understand 100% what is expected when it locates a target odor and allow it to practice those behaviors, so they become hardwired into the brain. I liken the detection to response sequence to a moth flying towards the light: it cannot help itself.

What is the Plan, Exactly?

After passing the Progress Check for Lesson 10, you are now ready to introduce the scent containers. These containers are distinct from primary and intermediate containers used to store and transport odors. These containers will be placed on the floor for the dog to interact with during training. I like to use a container with a low odor, such as glass or stainless-steel (for example, mason jars with mesh screen lids, or stainless-steel spice shakers which have lids with holes punched through).

The first stage is to teach the dog that the containers on the floor are productive and worth investigating. To conduct the transfer to the container we use the KONG piece and, in the first step, one container without a lid. The dog gets rewarded first for sniffing the container, then for sniffing and sitting. Additional containers are added in the lineup, then lids as the dog understands the container is productive to investigate.

Once you have the behavior of sniffing the container and giving a response, we need to add the target odor. The dog continues the sniff-sit-reward pattern, but now the target odor is part of the scent picture. If you do not have, or know, your target odor you can continue with the training plan using KONG. Then, once you have acquired your target odor you can repeat the training from this point forward to introduce the target.

Once you have the behavior of sniffing the target odor and giving a response, we need to proof it and also introduce discrimination training. Initially this will involve the use of interferents and the introduction of choices before adding to the complexity of the target odor presentations. Up to this point, the dog has had just one choice, and as long as it conducted a specific behavior, it was rewarded. Now we are starting to introduce the concept that rewardable behavior can only be triggered by the scent of a target odor.

You may find the dog approaches a blank container and gives a response. This is not unusual, and just shows the dog is repeating a previously rewarded behavior. Extinction is by far the best approach to resolve this behavior (see Terminology). Do not be tempted to get involved and show the dog what to do. If you do, the risk is that the dog may learn that when it is struggling to resolve an issue, it can just wait for the human to help it. We want to develop a detection dog prepared to resolve the problems encountered during detection and not to rely on the human all the time.

If the dog is becoming stressed and showing persistent displacement behaviors, it is best to stop the session. Give the dog a break, do some problem solving to see if you need to adjust your approach, then go back to training.

Once the dog has learned to differentiate between the target container and blank container, we add a second blank container. While it is advantageous for the dog to search the three containers in the order of blank then blank and then respond to the target, this order of events will not always occur because you will be moving the target odor container around and will not be directing the dog to search in a particular order. This is important—do not cue your dog toward any particular container. So, the search pattern will not necessarily be sequential with two blank containers and then one target odor container (in this exact order). However, as long as the dog is searching containers and giving the correct response, it is acceptable. At this point, we want to develop confidence and understanding of the game, and that involves the dog learning how to play "detection."

Ensure you move the containers around after each trial, so they are not in the same position all of the time. If you have an assistant to do this for you, this makes it easier. Also, wear gloves and avoid handling the target odor container then the other containers without changing gloves in between. Otherwise, you may transfer the target odor to blank containers.

We will now introduce the Odor Recognition Test (ORT) type arrangement, which is a linear arrangement of containers proceeding directly away from the dog/handler. There is no specific advantage in using this system other than it provides a "more likely" search sequence and it acclimatizes the dogs to a standard ORT type setup. As the ORT is a common assessment for certification and competitions it does not harm to start the process of teaching the concept at this stage. However, it is not a requirement and you can place the containers out in any configuration you wish.

At this point, the dog is successfully passing over blank containers and indicating on the target container. Now you will start to add interferent odors, so the dog needs to discriminate which container holds the target odor and ignore the non-target odors. Initially, you want to introduce very low-level interferents as the aim is not to trick the dog into a false response. We want to train/coach the dog to understand the rules of the game and make the right choices. This is where the black and white behaviors are essential, and there is no gray. Low-level interferent odors include:

Paper
Cardboard (not from food packaging)
Cotton

Gauze
Disposable gloves (new/clean)
Metal washers

The aim of the low-level interferents is that they add a non-desirable odor for the dog to smell but will not elicit a response of any kind. The dog can then easily ignore the interferents, understanding that there is an opportunity, in one of the other containers, for a reward.

Once the dog has mastered ignoring low-level interferents, you increase the interferent odors value. High-level interferent odors include:

Hotdog
Kibble
Piece of a tennis ball
Coffee
Disposable gloves handled with clean hands (no target odor)

The higher-level interferents aim to add a more desirable odor for the dog to smell but will not elicit a response of any kind. The dog can then easily ignore the interferents, understanding that there is an opportunity, in one of the other containers, for a reward.

Imprinting is the opportunity for you to communicate clearly and effectively to the dog what you want it to respond to. By ensuring we establish communication of the target odor to the dog, then as you progress through training, you will find that the behaviors remain consistent and balanced. You will also find that detection rates of the target will be robust in real life searches and with a consistency of behaviors even in the most challenging of situations.

Shouldn't the Dog Be Searching?

This workbook is focused on one task: imprinting. In reality I typically train the systems of search throughout the 15-day imprinting phase, but during separate training sessions. This is because I do not use the target scent to train the systems of search; systems of search are taught as obedience exercises. In fieldwork or any kind of detection with dogs, the searching phase is a lot longer than the actual detection phase. A detection dog will go through its whole working life spending over 90% of the time searching and less than 10% of the time detecting. Yet people spend a lot of time on the odor phase and do not invest in the searching phase. Your training program should be 90% of the time training the search and 10% on the target odor. This means training the systems of search separate from the odor and as standalone behaviors. By doing so, you will have a dog that can search effectively, efficiently, and for the duration and respond to a target odor when encountered. For this reason, I train the behaviors separately and, for the majority of initial and maintenance training, without odor even being placed out. Teaching systems of search is a whole book on its own and will be a follow-on title.

The Three-Legged Stool Principle

I developed something I called the three-legged stool principle during the time of training the Mine Detection Dogs. This is the principle I have used ever since and, in my opinion, provides the dog a clear understanding of the scent picture and a balanced and stable platform from which odor work is based.

The three elements of the principle are:

- Discrimination
- Trace detection
- Generalization

Discrimination

Discrimination within the 3-legged stool is an imprint technique I use to present more complex scent pictures to the dog once it has learned the target scent. I find this discrimination method fine-tunes the dog's nose and allows it to understand how to identify the target odor when there is background "noise" of other odors. In real life, the dog can encounter target odors mixed with environmental smells purposely, from humans trying to conceal something, or naturally, such as a reptile target living in a wooded area. The baseline odor (target) is still the same; with discrimination the dog learns to look for that odor among layers of a wide variety of other odors.

With that in mind, I mix the target with other smells, often the interferents already used, so the dog distinguishes between target and interferents when they are separate and when they are mixed together. In this way, it is not merely the dog determining "yes" it is the target or "no" it is not, which happens when you have a line-up of a target and interferents in separate jars. The dog also has to understand that there is not always a black and white difference. The odor may be considered grey, but the response should be the same. A target is the target, no matter how it is presented or encountered.

Trace detection

I calibrate the dog's nose to both trace amounts and the larger amounts the dog may encounter in the field. This provides a spread of detection capability from very small to field representative quantities. One of the reasons is that the dog may only encounter a small amount of odor in the field and still needs to understand it is a productive opportunity to locate a source. Additionally, it conditions the dog to search in detail rather than locating an "easy" detectable odor all the time and therefore becoming lazy. I find this happens with hydrocarbon detection dogs because the odor is so volatile and easy for the dog to find. I have to put trace amounts out, or the dog never learns to search hard to find the source.

Generalization

Generalization is the exposure of the dog to different variations of the same sample type. As mentioned previously, I want to expose the dog to at least three variations of the same kind of odor. This generalization ensures the dog understands all variations of the target are an opportunity to receive a reward.

During the Mine Detection Dog project, we imprinted on only Yugoslav TNT, and dogs were experts in its detection. A problem arose when we worked the dogs on American TNT: the dogs showed no change in behavior during the training phase. After a rapid imprint session (using the same technique in this workbook), the dogs transferred to the new odor. I was confused by this, and I took a consultation from a scientist who specialized in dog detection; he explained the phenomenon of the "expert nose." The expert nose is when we calibrate the dogs so precisely that it can distinguish between the trained target odor and all other variations of the same odor. The concept of a dog requiring generalization is outlined in the research paper entitled *Olfactory Generalization in Detector Dogs*. The author's state: "using multiple target exemplars appears to be the most effective way to promote elemental processing and broaden the generalization gradient, whereas increasing the number of training instances with fewer exemplars can narrow the gradient, thereby increasing discrimination" (Moser, Bizo, & Brown, 2019).

In some cases, the ability to only detect specific targets can be advantageous, such as when doing a field survey for a three-toed box turtle and we want the dog to ignore all other variations of the box turtle. We can train the dog to detect only the three-toed species and ignore other species. But in other surveys, we may want the dog to detect the presence of all box turtles, so in this case, we need to train generalization to all variations within the species.

Proper Preparation

By now, you should realize that the imprinting process isn't complicated as long as you have prepared the process thoroughly. The importance of your odor source, how you handle and store it, and how you set up the imprint sessions contribute to success. Preparation and clear communication are the key and, in most cases, take more time than the actual imprinting. This isn't a fault in the system; it is a strength because robust preparation is critical to success. There is a saying (it may be a military saying) that "prior planning and preparation prevents poor performance." Some versions of this wise adage include little expletives, but the message is the same. If you've made it this far in the workbook, you're on the right track so let's get training!

Training Plan, Lesson 11

Lesson Overview			
Event	Imprint Training 1 – Introduction of scent containers	Day	10
		Lesson No.	11
Equipment	Clicker (or chosen marker) Treats Treat pouch or container Piece of KONG approximately 2" x 2" 3 scent containers		
Location	Indoor room with minimal distractions		
Duration	6 x 5 minutes		
Aim	To teach the dog the concept of to sit and stare at a KONG within the scent container Introduction of the search cue		
Objectives	To teach the dog the concept of sit and stare at a target within a scent container		
Prerequisite Lesson	Response Training 6 – Sit and stare at KONG	Prerequisite Lesson No.	10
Setup	Prepare treats selected for the training event. The dog should be off lead. Have the treats readily available either in a pouch or a container close to hand. Ensure clicker (marker) functions correctly. Ensure KONG is clean. Ensure scent container is a low odor material, such as stainless steel or glass, and is clean and safe to use. Have a bowl of water available in the training area.		
Remarks			
Quick Look			

Training Plan, Lesson 11 (pg. 2)

	Steps to Success
Step	**Action**
1	Place the KONG piece inside the scent container and place the scent container on the floor in the same area you have been using to develop the sit and stare response. Stand 3 feet away from the scent container with the dog at your side.
2	(9.1) Give the dog the cue* (see below note) to search the scent container without a lid. If it sniffs the opening, click and reward. If the dog approaches and sits, wait until it sniffs the opening of the scent container, then click and reward. Ensure the dog is sniffing the KONG when you click.
2	(9.2) Place two scent containers out: one blank and one with KONG about 3 feet apart. (see diagram on page 89) Give the dog the cue to search the scent containers. Allow the dog to sniff the blank scent container; if it responds, wait until it moves to the next scent container. When the dog sniffs the scent container with KONG, wait for a response, click and reward. If the dog approaches and sits without searching, wait for it to sniff the KONG, then click and reward.
2	(9.3) Place three scent containers out: two blank and one with KONG, about 3 feet away from each other. Give the dog the cue to search the scent containers. Allow the dog to sniff the blank scent containers; if it responds wait until it moves on. When the dog sniffs the scent container with KONG, wait for a response, click and reward. If the dog approaches and sits without searching, wait for it to sniff the KONG, click and reward.
2	(9.4) Place the three scent containers out but WITH lids, about 3 feet from each other. Give the dog the cue to search. When the dog sniffs and give a sit response at the scent container with KONG, click and reward. If this step is too challenging, then reset by clicking on sniff. Then move to waiting for a response.
2	(9.5) Give the dog the cue to search the scent containers WITH lids. When the dog sniffs, gives a sit response, and holds the response for 3 seconds, then click. Ensure the dog is staring at the scent container when you click.
3	Repeat step 2, completing the number of repetitions specified for the subtask in the progression plan below. Once your dog has successfully completed two sessions (with breaks), move to the next subtask.

* Note: A cue word may be "seek", "find" or anything you chose to communicate to the dog to search.

Training Plan, Lesson 11 (pg. 3)

Progression Plan			
Task	Subtask	Description	Number of treats/clicks
9		**Sit and stare at the scent container with KONG**	
	9.1	Dog approaches scent container without a lid and sniffs the opening	3
	9.2	Dog searches two scent containers without lids, sniffs the openings, and gives a sit response at KONG	4
	9.3	Dog searches three scent containers without lids, sniffs opening, and gives a sit response at KONG	3
	9.4	Dog searches three scent containers WITH lids, sniffs, and gives a sit response to the correct container	3
	9.5	Dog searches three scent containers WITH lids, sniffs, and holds a sit response at the correct container for 3 seconds	4

Progress Check	
Does the dog sit for and stare for 3 seconds, having sniffed the scent container with a lid and containing KONG?	Yes/No
If no, repeat from 9.2 and reassess.	

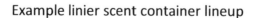

Example linier scent container lineup

Training Plan, Lesson 12

Lesson Overview			
Event	Imprint Training 2 – Introduction of target odor	Day	11
		Lesson No.	12
Equipment	Clicker (or chosen marker) Treats Treat pouch or container Target odor Piece of KONG approximately 2" x 2" Two scent containers for the odor (one for KONG, one for target odor)		
Location	Indoor room with minimal distractions		
Duration	6 x 5 minutes		
Aim	To teach the dog to sit and stare at a target odor		
Objectives	To teach the dog the concept of sit and stare at a target odor with duration		
Prerequisite Lesson	Imprint Training 1 – Introduction of scent containers	Prerequisite Lesson No.	11
Setup	Prepare treats selected for the training event. The dog should be off lead. Have the treats readily available either in a pouch or a container close to hand. Ensure clicker (marker) functions correctly. Ensure scent containers are clean and safe to use and contain the appropriate odor. Have a bowl of water available in the training area.		
Remarks			

Training Plan, Lesson 12 (pg. 2)

	Steps to Success
Step	**Action**
1	(10.1) Place the KONG piece inside a scent container (with lid on) and the scent container on the floor in the same area you have been using to develop the sit and stare response. Give the dog the cue to search. When the dog approaches the container, sniffs the top, and gives a sit response, click and reward.
1	(10.2) From this point forward you **DO NOT** place a scent container with KONG out at the same time as you have a target scent out. Place a scent container, holding **target odor** but no KONG, on the floor with the lid on. Give the dog the cue to search. If the dog approaches and sniffs the top, click and reward. If the dog approaches and sits, wait for it to sniff the top, then click and reward. Ensure the dog is sniffing the top of the container when you click.
1	(10.3) Place a scent container, holding **target odor** on the floor with the lid on. Give the dog the cue to search. When the dog approaches, sniffs, gives a sit response, and holds it for 3 seconds, click and reward. Ensure the dog is staring at the scent container when you click.
2	Repeat step 1, completing the number of repetitions specified for the subtask in the progression plan below. Once your dog has successfully completed two sessions (with breaks), move to the next subtask.

		Progression Plan	
Task	**Subtask**	**Description**	**Number of treats/clicks**
10		**Sit and stare at the scent container with the target odor**	
	10.1	Dog approaches scent container (KONG), sniffs and sits.	1
	10.2	Dog approaches scent container (target odor) and sniffs the top.	5
	10.3	Dog approaches scent container (target odor), sniffs top and holds a sit response for 3 seconds.	6

Progress Check	
Does the dog sit for and stare for 3 seconds, having sniffed the scent container with target odor?	Yes/No
If no, repeat from 10.2 and reassess.	

Training Plan, Lesson 13

Lesson Overview			
Event	Imprint Training 3 – Initial proofing, step 1	Day	12
		Lesson No.	13
Equipment	Clicker (or chosen marker) Treats Treat pouch or container Target odor 3 Scent containers: 1 for the odor and 2 clean (blanks)		
Location	Indoor room with minimal distractions		
Duration	4 x 5 minutes		
Aim	To confirm the dog's ability to recognize and detect the target odor		
Objectives	To confirm the dog's detection of the target odor To provide a basic introduction to searching behaviors		
Prerequisite Lesson	Imprint Training 2 – Introduction of target odor	Prerequisite Lesson No.	12
Setup	Prepare treats selected for the training event. The dog should be off lead. Have the treats readily available either in a pouch or a container close to hand. Ensure clicker (marker) functions correctly. Ensure blank scent containers are clean. Ensure scent container for odor is clean and contains target odor. Have a bowl of water available in the training area.		
Remarks			

Steps to Success	
Step	Action
1	Place the scent container with target odor on the floor in the same area you have been using to develop the sit and stare response. Place one blank container 3 foot away from the target scent container.
2	Give the dog the cue to search. Allow it to search in any order it wishes. If the dog responds on the blank scent container, ignore it and wait it out. Once it sniffs the target odor scent container, wait for a response and click after 3 seconds.
2	Give the dog the cue to search. Allow it to search in any order it wishes. If the dog responds on the blank scent container, ignore it and wait it out. Once it sniffs the target odor scent container, wait for a response and click after 5 seconds.
3	Repeat step 2, completing the number of repetitions specified for the subtask in the progression plan below. Once your dog has successfully completed two sessions (with breaks), move to the next subtask.

Progression Plan			
Task	Subtask	Description	Number of treats/clicks
11		**Initial proofing – Step 1**	
	11.1	The dog searches 2 scent containers and responds to the target odor for 3 seconds.	4
	11.2	The dog searches 2 scent containers and responds to the target odor for 5 seconds.	3

Progress Check	
Does the dog search 2 scent containers and sit and stare for 5 seconds at the target?	Yes/No
If no, repeat from 11.1 and reassess.	

Training Plan, Lesson 14

Lesson Overview			
Event	Imprint Training 4 – Initial proofing, step 2	Day	13
		Lesson No.	14
Equipment	Clicker (or chosen marker) Treats Treat pouch or container Target odor 3 Scent containers: 1 for the odor and 2 clean (blanks)		
Location	Indoor room with minimal distractions		
Duration	4 x 5 minutes		
Aim	To confirm the dog's ability to recognize and detect the target odor		
Objectives	To confirm the dog's detection of the target odor To provide a basic introduction to searching behaviors		
Prerequisite Lesson	Imprint Training 3 – Initial proofing, step 1	Prerequisite Lesson No.	13
Setup	Prepare treats selected for the training event. The dog should be off lead. Have the treats readily available either in a pouch or a container close to hand. Ensure clicker (marker) functions correctly. Ensure blank scent containers are clean. Ensure scent container for odor is clean and contains target odor. Have a bowl of water available in the training area.		
Remarks			

Training Plan, Lesson 14 (pg. 2)

	Steps to Success
Step	**Action**
1	Place the scent container with target odor on the floor in the same area you have been using to develop the sit and stare response. Place 2 blank containers at least 3 feet away from each other in a linear pattern.
2	Give the dog the cue to search. If the dog responds on a blank scent container, ignore it and wait it out. Once it sniffs the target odor scent container, wait for a response and click after 5 seconds. Rearrange the scent containers.
2	Give the dog the cue to search. If the dog responds on the blank scent container, ignore it and wait it out. Once it sniffs the target odor scent container, wait for a response and click after 7 seconds. Rearrange the scent containers.
3	Repeat step 2, completing the number of repetitions specified for the subtask in the progression plan below. Once your dog has successfully completed two sessions (with breaks), move to the next subtask.

	Progression Plan		
Task	**Subtask**	**Description**	**Number of treats/clicks**
12		**Initial proofing – Step 2**	
	12.1	The dog searches 3 scent containers and responds to the target odor for 5 seconds.	3
	12.2	The dog searches 3 scent containers and responds to the target odor for 7 seconds.	2

Progress Check	
Does the dog search three scent containers and sit and stare for 7 seconds at the target?	Yes/No
If no, repeat from 12.1 and reassess.	

Training Plan, Lesson 15

Lesson Overview			
Event	Imprint Training 5 – Initial proofing, step 3	Day	14
		Lesson No.	15
Equipment	Clicker (or chosen marker) Treats Treat pouch or container Target odor 3 Scent containers: 1 for the odor and 2 clean **Low-level** interferent odors (see description in Chapter 7)		
Location	Indoor room with minimal distractions		
Duration	4 x 5 minutes		
Aim	To confirm the dog's ability to recognize and detect the target odor when placed out with interferent odors		
Objectives	To confirm the dog's detection of the target odor To introduce the dog to interferent discrimination To provide a basic introduction to searching behaviors		
Prerequisite Lesson	Imprint Training 4 – Initial proofing, step 2	Prerequisite Lesson No.	14
Setup	Prepare treats selected for the training event. The dog should be off lead. Have the treats readily available either in a pouch or a container close to hand. Ensure clicker (marker) functions correctly. Ensure 2 interferent scent containers are clean and contain interferents. Ensure scent container for odor is clean and contains target odor. Have a bowl of water available in the training area.		
Remarks			

Steps to Success	
Step	**Action**
1	Place the scent container with an odor on the floor. Place two interferent scent containers, with an odor in each, at least 3 feet apart in a linear position in front of you.
2	Give the dog the cue to search. If the dog responds on an interferent scent container, ignore it and wait it out. Once it sniffs the target odor scent container, wait for a response and click after 3 seconds. Rearrange the scent containers.
2	Give the dog the cue to search. If the dog responds on the interferent scent container, ignore it and wait it out. Once it sniffs the target odor scent container, wait for a response and click after 7 seconds. Rearrange the scent containers.
3	Repeat step 2, completing the number of repetitions specified for the subtask in the progression plan below. Once your dog has successfully completed two sessions (with breaks), move to the next subtask.

Progression Plan			
Task	**Subtask**	**Description**	**Number of treats/clicks**
13		**Initial proofing – Step 3**	
	13.1	The dog searches 3 scent containers and responds to the target odor for 3 seconds.	2
	13.2	The dog searches 3 scent containers and responds to the target odor for 7 seconds.	1

Progress Check	
Does the dog search 3 scent containers and sit and stare for 7 seconds on the target, ignoring low-level interferents?	Yes/No
If no, repeat from 13.1 and reassess.	

Training Plan, Lesson 16

Lesson Overview			
Event	Imprint Training 6 – Initial proofing, step 4	Day	15
		Lesson No.	16
Equipment	Clicker (or chosen marker) Treats Treat pouch or container Target odor 3 Scent containers: 1 for the odor and 2 clean **High-level** interferent odors (see description in Chapter 7)		
Location	Indoor room with minimal distractions		
Duration	4 x 5 minutes		
Aim	To confirm the dog's ability to recognize and detect the target odor when placed out with interferent odors		
Objectives	To confirm the dog's detection of the target odor To proof the dog to interferent discrimination		
Prerequisite Lesson	Imprint Training 5 – Initial proofing, step 3	Prerequisite Lesson No.	15
Setup	Prepare treats selected for the training event. The dog should be off lead. Have the treats readily available either in a pouch or a container close to hand. Ensure clicker (marker) functions correctly. Ensure interferent scent containers are clean and contain interferents. Ensure scent container for odor is clean and contains target odor. Have a bowl of water available in the training area.		
Remarks			

Training Plan, Lesson 16 (pg. 2)

Steps to Success	
Step	**Action**
1	Place the scent container with target odor on the floor. Place 2 interferent scent containers, with an interferent in each, at least 3 feet apart in a linear position in front of you.
2	Give the dog the cue to search. If the dog responds on an interferent scent container, ignore it and wait it out. Once it sniffs the target odor scent container, wait for a response and click after 5 seconds. Rearrange the scent containers.
2	Give the dog the cue to search. If the dog responds on an interferent scent container, ignore it and wait it out. Once it sniffs the target odor scent container, wait for a response and click after 7 seconds. Rearrange the scent containers.
3	Repeat step 2, completing the number of repetitions specified for the subtask in the progression plan below. Once your dog has successfully completed two sessions (with breaks), move to the next subtask.

Progression Plan			
Task	**Subtask**	**Description**	**Number of treats/clicks**
14		**Initial proofing – Step 4**	
	14.1	The dog searches 3 scent containers and responds to the target odor for 5 seconds.	2
	14.2	The dog searches 3 scent containers and responds to the target odor for 7 seconds.	1

Progress Check	
Does the dog search 3 scent containers and sit and stare for 7 seconds on the target, ignoring high-level interferents?	Yes/No
If no, repeat from 14.1 and reassess.	

Congratulations! Your dog is imprinted to a target odor and will ignore interferents while conducting a basic search then give a response when detected!

However, this is just the start, and the training process doesn't stop there. Now you must consolidate all this learning and prove the dog in a variety of situations. But at this point, you and your dog are ready to do that.

If you have been concurrently training your dog in systems of search, you are ready to integrate the two methods and develop your detection dog's capability.

You should continue working on Task Number 14, but change the following: interferents, location for training, heights of the scent containers, scent containers, and also add distractions such as environmental sounds. Further, change the quantity of the target odor you are hiding and the age of the target odor (if relevant). Proof the behaviors in as many different ways that you can BUT only change one thing at a time. Do not overwhelm the dog by making too many changes in the training scenario.

NOTES

CHAPTER 8 – RECORD KEEPING

In general, I have found that dog trainers are poor record keepers. I believe the practical nature of the tasks involved in dog training lends to the collective dislike of doing the paperwork. I admit that I am one of those people and recognize that I do need to stay on top of my records and not let them get away from me. It is essential to maintain your training records and ensure you complete them as your training progresses. Do not try to recall on a Friday what you did on a Monday. However, it is a lot easier nowadays to use technology to help keep your records up to date. Easy-to-use smartphone apps are available and capture a lot of important data without too much input at the time of training. Because I do more research-based training than anything, I have a commercial software system that allows me to develop records specific to the task and record fieldwork. This custom-coded software program automatically collects climate data (even inside the training lab) as well as location, time and date; all from a small weather meter. This data is then transferred into the record. The software will also read barcodes of the target and interferent odors, so the contents of any container details are automatically added to the record. However, this comes at a cost and is probably outside the requirements of a typical detection team.

A potential solution that I beta tested, and due to be released in 2021, is Logs4Dogs (www.logs4dogs.com). This app can be used on mobile devices and, once set up via the web-based software, tracks your dog's progress. It is designed for step-by-step training plans such as this one and tracking your progress much faster and easier than paper records. The customizable software provides the ability to track progress and establish Progress Checks to ensure you are reaching the milestones and progressing according to the plan. The app collects data at the time of the training event, including the results, allowing for analyzing the training and meeting your training goals.

Maintaining training records allows you to monitor progress and trends, especially if things are not going the way your plan expected. They provide a clear record of the steps taken, and you may see where training has hit a bump and, therefore, what needs to be adjusted. Additionally, it will assist in the future development of training plans as you can determine the time taken to train specific tasks and how you can adapt from the lessons learned. In some cases, training records are a requirement, such as for dog teams certified with particular organizations. Whether you use paper or digital records, it is beneficial to have a system to record your training data.

The records do not have to be a complicated affair. Even a simple checklist to record progress is better than no record at all. It will keep you on track and prevent any confusion as to where you are in the process. The use of an app is excellent as it can record a lot of information automatically and all you need to do is press a button to confirm the training standard was met or not. This is especially true during imprinting as the process is so sequential and progressive but not complicated.

The way I was able to develop the imprinting system in this workbook was from record keeping. Over time I could analyze the data and see, in general, what it took to complete each phase for a bunch of dogs. The collected data then provided an accurate timeline, which I could use to estimate training duration across the full spectrum of tasks the dog must be trained in. So, when someone asks, "how long to train a dog to do this?" I can accurately estimate. When I produce a detection dog training plan, imprinting is always 15 days.

CONCLUSION

Remember, this journey should be enjoyable and rewarding. Each stage should progress from the one before. It is important to maintain the approach that the dog is setting the pace of the learning. There will be steps or even whole sections in this process that you may feel you can add your tweak. That is fine! Find what works for you, your training style, your methodology, your prior experiences, and most importantly, your dog.

Do not forget to check out the workbook resources page on my website regularly, as I will post updates, videos, and relevant scientific papers/articles to keep you informed.

One of the most critical stages is reward selection. I hope you and your dog enjoyed this exercise, and maybe you even learned some things about your dog. It's a fun, rewarding, and informative assessment and pays dividends in the long run. It is worth repeating every so often, I recommend monthly as part of your routine maintenance. This is my recommendation even with a trained dog. You can use the hierarchy of rewards in maintenance training to assist in:

- Meeting your required standards
- Maintaining your required standards
- Advancing your required standards

Because now you have a very powerful tool to assist you, a reward hierarchy!

Once a dog is conditioned to the clicker (or any marker), it is a versatile and valuable tool to keep in the toolbox. Again, maintenance training includes the clicker for the same three reasons above. Imprinting is just one element in the detection dog's repertoire, and the clicker can support a lot of other training techniques. I only utilize the clicker for the training of a behavior. Once a behavior is taught and reliable on cue; verbal, hand signal, whistle, or independent stimuli such as a target odor, the click is no longer needed. The clicker is a great way to communicate, and isn't that one of the essential skills in training dogs? The ability to communicate!

I hope now you have an understanding of how vital your selection, use, and storage of target odor is. We are talking about communication with the dog and how important that is. If the dog does not understand the target odor because it was taught using a confusing set of irrelevant odors, it will not be effective or efficient in the field. By ensuring we have been diligent in odor selection and then careful in its storage and handling, we are achieving the aim of clear communication of what we want the dog to find. Low-quality samples can lead to issues, but the incorrect handling and storage of very good samples will lead to contamination and confusion. We know from the research that having a baseline of contamination of your training aids throughout the training area will communicate to the dog to ignore trace amounts of target odors (DeChant, Bunker, & Hall, 2021).

The sequence of imprinting isn't complicated, as hopefully, you can now see. It's a progressive plan of steps that sequentially move one to the next. We set small criteria gates through which the dog must pass to progress, and if it doesn't, we reset the training and ensure it understands the task. With each training session, you must ensure you know the goal and stick to it. By having a defined training goal and working on the plan, you will find that training progresses faster and provides a quality of learning. If the dog does not reach the training goal then stop, reset and try again, either immediately or after a break. The dog's world is run by scent more than sight; therefore, we are just taking what is natural to the dog and adding some criteria to the process. By asking the dog to indicate (sit, stand, stare, bark, or whatever you choose) at a given target odor to receive a reward, we are just entering the dog's world for a short period to enable us to achieve an aim. Over the decades, I have imprinted hundreds of dogs, and I have also utilized many different systems to do that. In the end, this imprinting process is the one I have found produces the most reliable, consistent, and fastest imprinted dogs because it is based on clear communication.

Keeping records of training is essential. I keep very detailed records that include climatic conditions to include temperature, humidity, pressure, wind speed, direction, plus the usual time, date, location, and details as you see in the progression plan. I use software to do the record-keeping as it takes a lot less time, and most of the details are completed automatically. This level of data collection isn't always needed, but the significant parts contained in the progress plans included in this workbook are encouraged as a part of the data you should capture for your own records. But don't let it stop at the end of imprinting. Maintaining your records to capture all of your training data will help in the long run. Especially if you are looking for trends in specific training issues or even when deployed in the field. Do not rely on memory; it often fades quicker than it recalls.

I will be releasing a workbook to cover the aspects of directional and working control you will need to conduct searches. The aim is to create a companion to the imprinting workbook so that you can take the imprinted dog into the field and conduct surveys/searches efficiently, effectively, and successfully. You can have the greatest imprinted dog in the world, but if you cannot handle him into productive areas, he will never be close enough to a target odor to find it. I sometimes hear the question; What is more important, the ability to search or respond on target? To me, it is the ability to search! If a dog cannot search effectively, then it can never find an odor even to respond. If I am watching the dog and understand its communication, then even a slight change of behavior is enough for me to investigate an area or location. But ideally, we want a dog that is capable of both skill sets, search and respond. This workbook provided you the response and imprinting to odor skills; next is the searching. Importantly you must remember to:

Train the dog in front of you!

REFERENCES

API, *Canine Oil Detection: Field Trials Report*. American Petroleum Institute, Technical Report 1149-3, Washington DC, 2016 https://chiron-k9.com/wp-content/uploads/2017/08/canine-oil-detection-field-trials-report.pdf

DeChant, M. T., Bunker, P. C., & Hall, N. J. *Stimulus Control of Odorant Concentration: Pilot Study of Generalization and Discrimination of Odor Concentration in Canines*. Animals, 11(2), 326, 2021 doi:10.3390/ani11020326

Duranton, C., & Horowitz, A. *Let me sniff! nosework induces positive judgment bias in pet dogs*. Applied Animal Behaviour Science, 211, 61-66, 2019. doi:10.1016/j.applanim.2018.12.009

Gad, S. *Encyclopedia of Toxicology*. Trinitrotoluene, 855-857, 2014. doi:10.1016/b978-0-12-386454-3.00957-x

Moser AY, Bizo L, Brown WY. *Olfactory Generalization in Detector Dogs*. Animals. 2019; 9(9):702. https://doi.org/10.3390/ani9090702

Owens, E.H., Bunker, P. and Taylor, E., *K9 SCAT Subsurface Oil Detection and Delineation Field Study on Coarse-Sediment Beaches in Prince William Sound, Alaska*. Proc. 41st AMOP Technical Seminar on Environmental Contamination and Response, ECCC, Ottawa ON, 2018.

Owens, E.H., Dubach, H.C, Bunker, P., MacDonald, S., Yang, Z., Lambert, P. and Laforest, S., *Canine Oil Detection (K9-SCAT) following 2015 Releases from the T/V Arrow Wreck*. Proceedings International Oil Spill Conference, American Petroleum Institute, Washington DC. Vol, 2017, No. 1, 2620-2641, 2017. http://ioscproceedings.org/doi/pdf/10.7901/2169-3358-2017.1.2620

ABOUT THE AUTHOR

I live in San Antonio, Texas, USA, although I am originally from the United Kingdom. I was raised with dogs and naturally transitioned from school into the British Army to become a dog trainer.

I started my professional training career in 1982 when I enlisted and joined the Royal Army Veterinary Corps (RAVC) as a dog trainer. Initially, I served my apprenticeship training Patrol (attack) dogs before completing an advanced trainer's course and moving into canine detection. We would place live explosives inside metal or plastic tubes in those early days and throw them for the dog to fetch. There were no standardized construction methods, and whatever we had on hand was used to make the tubes. The dogs were also encouraged to respond by actively digging at the source of that target. Disposable gloves were never worn, and explosives were handled with bare hands. Since C4 gave me raging headaches, I would always use something to prevent direct skin contact. When I think back to those days, I cringe at just how little we knew. In 1998 I attended an Association of Chief Police Officers (ACPO) Explosive Detection Dog Trainers course at Mount Browne Police Headquarters, Guildford, England. It was on this course that I first saw, and trained with, passive response detection dogs. The passive response is the method of alerting on a trained target odor without touching it. On return to the military dog training school, I attempted to adopt the passive system, but this was met with some reluctance. However, a series of consequences happened in 1999 that started the journey of change. The military dog school had received a request to train members of the Australian Army Corps of Engineers in off-leash Explosive Dog Detection. One of their requirements was that the dogs needed to be trained in passive response and not be active on the target odor. At the time, I was the Senior Non-Commissioned Officer (NCO) in-charge of detection dog training. This was a perfect opportunity to develop our training system for the passive response. It was later in 1999 that I was put in charge of a special project to train Mine Detection Dogs (termed Explosive Detection Dogs – EDD, in the British military due to a concern of public perception). The very nature of landmine detection meant that a passive response was critical, and so the integration of the system into military training became a requirement, not a desire. The freedom afforded me by the Officer-in-Charge, Major Matt Sheriff, meant there was a lot of research and development of ideas throughout the project. This included, but was not limited to, the introduction of the clicker into training (more about that in Chapter 3), training the dogs to detect trace amounts of the target (0.025gm/ 0.00088 of TNT), working on aged, buried targets and a 6-minute passive response. Nowadays, these appear fairly common standards, but back then, it was groundbreaking work. The journey continued with setting up the US Army's Corps of Engineers Mine Detection Dog program, the Department of Defenses Specialized Search Dog (SSD) program, which included introducing the passive response (termed Deferred Final Response – DFR, in the US military) as well as other programs.

In 2014 I attended an oil spill response conference and met Dr. Ed Owens, a world-renowned expert in the field. We discussed the concept of Oil Detection Canines, and a plan was drawn up on a paper napkin, literally. The next year we completed a research trial into a dog's effectiveness to locate oil up to 3-feet (1 meter) below the surface (API, 2016). Having proven the concept, opportunities to deploy with the assets to Nova Scotia, Canada (Owens et al., 2017), Prince William Sound, Alaska (Owens and Bunker, 2018), and Newcastle, Wyoming affirmed the capability in a real-world environment. In 2016, an extensive pipeline oil spill impacted a river in Saskatchewan, Canada, and once again, the teams deployed to support the response effort. The teams had over 10,000 confirmed alerts on oil in vegetation, shoreline, debris wracks, and even underwater while working six days a week for four months. The experience underlined the need for robust imprinting and proved that this work requires dogs that can maintain motivation for 6 hours searching and locating up to 183 targets in a day. Over the decades, this extensive training and field experience honed my system and provided real data to support its effectiveness, even in the most hostile environments and challenging situations.

In 2017 I started my canine consultancy and training company, Chiron K9, LLC. It had always been my desire to train and handle dogs for conservation and environmental detection projects, and from the very start, that has been my company's focus. Also, I love research into canine detection capabilities and wanted to be involved with the science side of training. One of the advantages of working for yourself is that no one is there telling you how you must do things. The freedom to train how I wanted to, try out new techniques, and research new ideas meant I could develop systems of training that worked based on all the years of experience I had gained.

Having said all that, I have had challenges in imprinting along the way. After training hundreds of dogs, you cannot expect it to go perfect every time. Some dogs need extra work and require us to break the steps down even further than in this workbook. That is perfectly fine—every dog is an individual, and we must train the dog that is in front of us. You know your dog better than I do, so if you know something works better for your dog, then use it. The workbook provides flexibility in the actual training steps to apply the techniques needed to ensure success and that you progress in sequence.

CONNECT WITH THE AUTHOR

Have you enjoyed the book? Would you like to stay in touch with me and keep the conversation flowing? Fabulous!

I have lots of freebies to share with you, which might just help you, including extra copies of the forms used for record keeping, videos, and research I have been involved in.

AND if you'd like to join my private Facebook community that's all about imprinting your dog and spend time with like-minded people who are going through the same journey as you, then you'd be most welcome. I would love to see photos of you, your dog, and the workbook posted to the Facebook group. Let me know how you got on and ask questions if you need some guidance or support.

You will find all sorts of information on the workbook's media page:

www.Chiron-K9.com/imprinting-book

Please consider writing a review.

I enjoy teaching seminars, workshops, and presentations and I am happy to travel and meet new people and, of course, their dogs. If you feel some practical training would benefit, please reach out and see what we can arrange.

Instagram: @ChironK9
Facebook: www.facebook.com/ChironK9LLC
YouTube: www.YouTube.com/ChironK9

Printed in Great Britain
by Amazon

17507832R00063